Every Entrepreneurs Guide: Running Your Own Business

Research: James Miller, Helen Sykes, Peter Guthridge, Mark Gregory and Shawn Willis

Edited By Kizzi Nkwocha (c)

Originally published in 2016.

This third edition is published by Athena Publishing in 2018

Sponsored by The Cryptocurrency Magazine
(www.thecryptocurrencymagazine.com)

Also by Mithra and Athena Publishing

Escape Your 9-5 And Do Something Amazing

Customer Service

SocMed: Social Media For Business

How To Start A Business With Little Or No Cash

Facebook For Business

Social Media Marketing: Write Up your Tweet

Getting Your Business LinkedIn

It's That Easy! Online Marketing 3.0

Business, Business, Business!

Mind Your Own Business

Insiders Know-how: Running A PR Agency

Insiders Know-how: Caring For Your Horse

Energy Efficiency

Social PR

Every Entrepreneurs Guide:

RUNNING YOUR OWN

BUSINESS

CONTRIBUTING AUTHORS

James Blake, Paul Stallard, Susan Wilkin, Nerida Mills,Tara Geraghty, Tabitha Jean Naylor, Trish Springsteen, Eddie Blass, Rune Sovndahl, Katina Beveridge, Alex Packham, Lisa Pantelli , Adam Tavener, Dianna Jacobsen Orsolya Bartalis and Gary Turner.

CONTENTS

Introduction

The very nature of being an entrepreneur and an innovator means that you fully embrace ambiguity and are comfortable with being challenged regularly. Choosing this career path is completely irrational because the odds of succeeding are dismal, but most succeed because of their unwavering belief, laser focus on delivering and persistence.

Starting a company, or managing a company through a period of transition and growth, can be a riveting roller coaster of emotions with tremendous highs and at times, difficult lows.

The purpose of this book is to help you ride out the storms and to avoid those costly, time-consuming mistakes that can mean the difference between success and failure.

Is running your own business worth the effort? A lot depends on your purpose in setting up the business. Do you want the freedom of working for yourself; to create something tangible; make a good living; to do something worthwhile or to make a fortune? If you answer yes to any of these questions then it most definitely is worth the effort.

Managing your own business is a difficult road full of unexpected twists and turns. I hope that this book makes that journey a much easier one. Every Entrepreneurs Guide: Running Your Own Business is the long-awaited revision and update of our fantastic business guide, Insiders Know-How: Running Your Own Business.

It's taken three years to update the Insiders Guide with many new chapters and topics. I know you'll love the result.

Here's to your success.

Kizzi Nkwocha

Publisher, My Entrepreneur Magazine and The Property Investor

About Kizzi Nkwocha

Kizzi Nkwocha is a publicist and the publisher of My Entrepreneur Magazine, Gold Oil and Diamonds Magazine and The Property Investor. As a widely respected and successful media consultant Nkwocha has represented a diverse range of clients including the King of Uganda, mistresses of President Clinton, Amnesty International, Pakistani cricket captain Wasim Akram, campaign group Jubilee 2000, Dragons Den businessman, Levi Roots and world record teenage sailor, Michael Perham.

Nkwocha has also become a well-known personality on both radio and television. He has been the focus of a Channel 4 documentary on publicity and has hosted his own talk show, London Line, on Sky TV. Nkwocha now runs a successful consultancy managing PR for businesses and individuals. His consultancy is at www.prhq.co.uk. Kizzi is the author of the book Heavens Fire and its sequel, The Prophecy of
The Popes, is due for release in June 2018.

Follow Kizzi on Twitter: https://twitter.com/kizzinkwocha

Starting a Business from Scratch: Challenges Faced and How to Overcome Them

James Blake

I. Introduction

It's hard running a start-up, it is all consuming, but it is also the most fun that you can possibly have. In order to be in charge of a start-up, you have to be prepared for any direction it may go and remain focused while going over every hurdle. You need to truly believe in your idea or innovation. If a business idea has a lot of earning potential but you do not love it, then you will never feel truly invested and it will never reach its maximum potential. If it is something that you love and you see the earning potential that others don't see yet, your passion is what will sell it.

I never thought that I would start my own business. I saw a future in the corporate world working for big companies, doing big deals, and earning big pay cheques. At the start of my career, I worked for a small business of around 30-40 people which I have always said (and believed) was the best experience to shape me and allowed me to succeed in my field. Small businesses are agile, intense, flexible, and much more exciting than big tanker corporates; this is what pushed me to take the leap and start my own company.

II. The Idea

The foundation of Hello Soda was as much of a shock to me as it was to anyone else. Looking back, what pushed me over the edge was my frustration.

It seemed obvious to me that, after the credit crunch, the world had changed. Credit data hadn't evolved since the late 70s to early 80s, yet the way we interacted with businesses had changed totally. We no longer did business face-to-face, everything was through apps or the internet which meant that companies lost touch with their customers and they no longer understood them as individuals.

I wanted corporations to take into account what really matters. Time and time again I saw people being given loans that they should not have been granted while other people were being rejected for loans that they needed and should have had. This wasn't because businesses were trying to be unreasonable but because necessary information (our likes, dislikes, spending habits, etc.) were not available through traditional data bureaus. However, this data was available through other sources and, while businesses had advanced to use social media to communicate with customers, none had begun to use social data to understand their customers and utilise it to their advantage.

Then came the idea; I had this revelation and I wanted to act on it. It was something I felt truly passionate about and something that I knew was important; to utilise social data for business decisions.

The first challenge arose when I realised that big companies, like the one I was in, were too happy with the current status quo and familiarity to implement such a large change. I realised that I couldn't put my idea into practice and stay in the big corporation, I had to leave.

III.   Leaving the Big Corporation

The first thing I did was to look for smaller businesses who were more flexible and creative to help consumers. I couldn't find any. My frustration grew so I decided that this was the test - "do I have the conviction to do it myself?" I spoke to a number of people and found that a couple of my colleagues shared my frustrations so, following 18 months of dreaming, we decided that we would take the jump together and start our own business.

What I learnt from this experience is that people get excited easily but they are mostly very scared of change; from investors, to team members and even co-founders, there was a huge amount of procrastination and one day it came down to two of us deciding that we had to do it and just see if others would join along the way. We found that, once our momentum began, others jumped on board. We were able to find investors who were willing to

support us to establish a small team of four people, but our next challenge was to convince very bright, driven individuals to join our journey when there was no guarantee that payroll could be met at the end of the month.

In my view, this is when it comes down to your belief in what you are doing, and communicating that belief. If you do not believe in the project, no-one else will; if you don't take more of a risk than everyone else, no one will follow your lead. You have to be the one to set an example. One of the principles I live by is: I get paid less and I get paid last. As the leader of a start-up business, you have a responsibility to the team, and to the shareholders, to prove that they did the right thing by investing in you and your idea.

Despite its difficulties, I find it easier running my own start-up business than I found working in the corporate world. Previously, I had treated every role I had as if it were my own business, which is why I was successful, but I struggled with the fact that sometimes I couldn't implement change or grow the business as fast as I wanted to because of ingrained processes or management structures. Now, I get to affect everything that I am involved in. I believe that you only feel pressure if you can't affect things yourself. That is why I love working in a start-up business. Each and every day, all of us can directly affect the outcome of the business.

One key difficulty with starting your own business is that there is nowhere to hide. If we let a client down, I feel as though I have let them down personally. If a team member feels unsupported or unfulfilled, it falls to me again. But when we grow, when things go well, and when we prove to a client that what we are doing is worthwhile and valuable, there is no greater feeling.

IV.   Finding the Right Team

The most important aspect of a successful start-up is hiring people better than yourself. If you are the expert at everything in your business, then you are doing something wrong and it will not grow. Encourage your team to be brave and go outside of their comfort zone. Let them make mistakes but ensure that they learn from these mistakes; innovation only comes from trial
and error. There is no such thing as a stupid question or suggestion. The only people who suffer from stupidity are those not brave enough to voice their own concerns or ideas.

To build a start-up team, you need creative, driven, delivery-focused people who want challenges. In other words, you want the best of the best, ambitious and brave! At Hello Soda, we look for three key things :
1) mind-set
2) skillset
3) structure.

The hardest of these to identify and improve is mind-set but it is also the most important. Everyone claims to have great work ethic and everyone says they can handle pressure, that they are driven, ambitious and like a challenge. But in reality, most people aren't driven, and most people don't really like a challenge. The key to success of start-up is finding individuals with right mind-set to tick these boxes. Skillset and structure can be taught.

I find it easy to recruit people with the right mind-set, because they are the only ones who would want to work in an environment as demanding and rewarding as a start-up. The people without it are usually scared off at the interview stage. Ask the important questions (to yourself first, and to potential team members after): Is this really what you want? If you are looking for a 9-5 role where you can hide or play golf or take Friday afternoons off without the boss knowing, this is not the role for you. If you are looking for a place where you can't see the effect of the work you do each day, this is not the place for you. But, if you want an environment that will challenge and support you, and believe in your ability no matter what experience or background you have, then there is no better environment to be.

V.   Managing Diverse Personalities

Another challenge for start-ups (in the tech space at least) is managing diverse personalities and skillsets in such a small area. In a big corporate company, the development team are on a different floor to the sales team, and the data science team sit away from all of them. In a start-up, everyone is together in the same room. You are small enough to be in the same building, but not big enough to have management layers so you have to communicate with people of diverse personalities from sales to software development. It is a fascinating insight into how businesses work when you see a developer frustrated at a sales person for being too loud, or a sales person's frustration at a developer for not communicating verbally.

Initially, it was difficult understanding that some people don't get excited about landing a big contract but do about solving a difficult data challenge. This challenge is made much easier if you find individuals with similar core values such as their drive and ambition .

VI.   Doing Something that has Never Been Done Before

When we began at Hello Soda, our focus was to empower consumers with their data footprint to allow them to receive goods and services they wanted at the right cost. It was turning unstructured, random data into structured, useful insights. Soon it became obvious that this had never been done before. We had no roadmap to follow and could not learn from others, we truly researched and developed from the very start.

We went live with our first client in 2013. There were high fives around the office, and pats on backs but, 24 hours later, the system had crashed.

What we proved to be very good at in the early days was reacting fast. Our customers supported us because we admitted when we were wrong and we lacked the arrogance that big companies can sometimes have. You have to always listen and be brave enough to change your mind and to say when you are wrong. However, the truth is that most people hate making decisions because they are scared to be wrong. Someone has to take the responsibility. That was the hardest thing for me to learn.

The key point was that our clients and partners knew that they were embarking on a journey with us that had never been done before. An analogy I use a lot is "Christopher Columbus didn't set out to discover America, he was looking for India, he just happened to bump into a new continent in between." When we solve one problem, we find more, and sometimes we find answers to questions that haven't even been asked yet by clients. That's the exciting part of working in a truly disruptive business, you set the goals and you have the flexibility to move.

I always struggle to tell people difficulties we faced. To be frank, I don't see them as difficulties - they were challenges and hurdles. Many of them were intellectual, some of them fiscal, but that's what everyone in this business wanted in their careers...to be challenged. There was a lot that we needed to learn: how to do payroll, how to complete tax, and how to rent out office space. The important thing was to keep long and medium term goals in focus, while understanding that what you do today is of the utmost importance.

I see a lot of start-ups with great ideas on a piece of paper, trying to raise investment, and I struggle to understand how they could even be classed as a business. You have to go out there and do something first, test ideas, sign up customers, test products and improve.

We are living through a time of serial start-up entrepreneurs. But I don't see myself as an entrepreneur, I don't think you can class yourself as one until you have achieved something. Just raising repeated rounds of money and delivering nothing is not entrepreneurial; Richard Branson or Bill Gates are entrepreneurs. Anyone can have an idea, but having the guts and ability to implement and build it is much more difficult.

VII.   Financial Difficulties

People have asked how I coped with the pressure of not knowing if there was a pay cheque at the end of the month. Cash flow is the biggest challenge for start-up businesses; you can have multiple clients, recurring revenue, and great invoice points, but what you don't realise is: not everyone will pay on time. You can budget but a tax bill can come in that you weren't expecting. Or someone might resign, meaning that you need to pay a recruitment fee to replace them. You might even have to fly to visit important clients, which wasn't in the budget.

One thing I guarantee any start-up is that your business plan will last, at best, three months. The banks want you to have one, but they'll also want you to be making £2m profit to lend you £300,000 and that isn't the world we live in. To survive and prosper, the ability to bend and be flexible for opportunity is vital. Our business plan was to focus on financial services, but we identified an opportunity in the consumer space and it became our biggest sector for a time. It allowed us to grow the team, it bought us time for our pipeline to close in some blue chip organisations, and it helped us learn that our products were multi-sector. There has never been a time in history more difficult for B2B start-ups than the one we live in today.

Our best target customers are huge blue chip multinational organisations with long procurement processes, consensus decision-making processes and teams specialising in ensuring the best price possible who utilise your need for cash flow to their advantage. Unless you are 100% confident in your value proposition, and you can demonstrate this to your clients, do not engage with those organisations. Otherwise, by the time you've come out of it, you would have spent more on resources than the deal is worth. Before we engaged with blue chip companies, we tested our proposition, understood its value, and were sure we would be confident in negotiations.

You should also be proud of the size and flexibility of your organisation. Some start-ups are ashamed of it but remember that innovation only comes in start-up businesses. Big businesses do not encourage innovations, it doesn't work. Many of these organisations are coming to realise that themselves. We have worked with a number of huge companies that have been wonderful and fair because they know that, without companies like us, innovation will die and they will not grow as a business. In my experience, if you have honesty and integrity and admit your mistakes, any business will support you; but don't try to be something you're not as they will see through it.

Managing resources takes great care and prioritisation. Knowing how to budget and how to get the most for your money is essential for successful resource management. The founders and directors are the last to be paid on a start-up and they get paid the least. Finally, we make sure to work with partners who believe in us and who believe in our mid-term outlook, not just anyone that will make us a quick buck.

VIII.   Remaining Positive

Your start-up may be a billion-dollar business in the making, you just have to get others to see that too. Without that first step of putting your careers and money on the line, it will remain just a dream. I really don't believe in fate, I believe that you make your own luck and you can control your destiny through hard work, and hard work only. You don't have to be the most talented or brilliant minded, but you do need a work ethic that most don't possess and a tenacity to be able to find your way through when there seems to be no path. When things get the most difficult, these are the moments when clarity is so important, these are the moments when I am at my calmest. You can't implement everything and you sometimes can't implement things even when you know they are correct because of circumstances.

Before embarking on a new business venture, you need to look at yourself in the mirror and ask "am I up for the fight? Is this something that is my passion and obsession, or is it a living?" If your answer is the latter, go and work for someone else. You will only be successful starting a business from scratch if you have total belief and clarity in what you are doing. You will make mistakes and things will go wrong, but plenty of people tell you that, not many people tell you the good things that you are doing. If you don't believe in yourself and your business, no one else will tell you that you're doing the right things. People will tell you never to doubt yourself but I don't agree, you should have doubts, you should challenge yourself and your decision-making process, just don't let anyone know that you do.

James Blake

About the author

James Blake is the founder and CEO of Hello Soda, a fast-growing international data-analytics company headquartered in Manchester, UK.

James was previously Head of Global Sales at Callcredit but since found a passion in making business personal again and left to build his own business. In less than three years, Hello Soda has grown from a small start-up with no funding or workspace, to having an international presence with offices in the UK and Bangkok and a team of 24.

Hello Soda is multisector and operates in the financial services, retail, HR, recruitment, insurance, and gaming sectors. It is well funded by European

Investors and James has ambitions to build £100m analytics software by 2021.

James is the proud father of two young children, he is a patriotic Welshman and a keen football fan. He is the first to initiate social activities with the team and truly believes that happy employees are the key to success.

The Power Of Story

Paul Stallard

People forget facts but remember stories.

That's why businesses need to put storytelling at the heart of everything they do to create emotional connections that shape how people perceive brands and compel them to interact with them.

Unless every story told is brutally focussed on a business outcome it is very easy to not get heard.

Enhancing reputations. Driving up sales. Winning hearts and minds. Creative storytelling makes an impact.

Start with a story

But before we delve into how you can apply storytelling to your business let's start with a story.

Sitting comfortably? Let us begin. The advertising copywriter did the same walk to work most days. A deep sense of sadness consumed him as he passed by an old man begging on the street corner. He noticed the beggar's tin was completely empty. Winter was on its way and donations had dried up. Next to the dented tin was a worn piece of cardboard bearing the old man's pitch: 'I am blind. Please give.'

The young man wanted to give money and often he did. But he wondered whether there was anything else he could do. It weighed heavily on his mind until inspiration came. He stopped and kneeled next to the old man and said, "My name is Peter. I would like to help you." The old man turned his head towards the sound of the helpful voice. "Would you object if I wrote a new message on your piece of cardboard?" "What have I got to lose? I haven't heard a single coin land today. Be my guest," said the old man.

Peter pulled out his black felt-tipped pen, turned the cardboard over and wrote down a single sentence. He neatly placed the cardboard back next to the tin, said his goodbyes and left. All morning, Peter wondered whether his idea had worked. He returned in his lunch hour where he found a much happier old man. It was hardly surprising. His tin was brimming with coins. "What did you write on my board? I am very grateful and very curious. But you never said and I have listened to coins land in my tin all morning." He read out the words that had inspired so many people to give. "Today is a beautiful sunny day. You can see it. But I cannot."

The blind beggar's story tells us how storytelling can inspire people to behave differently. While storytelling has become a buzzword in marketing circles, the subtleties of good storytelling have been lost somewhere along the way. Many businesses still think that stories extolling the virtues of a brand, or new products are just what an audience wants. But does it? Does anyone really care about your message, your brand, or how pleased you are to announce the launch of Version 2.0 of whatever product you are selling?

The mistake is thinking the story is about the product when really the best stories are the ones that involve the product. Let's say I wanted to engage your interest in my particular brand of washing powder. Do you want to know that it is concentrated, that it smells nice, that it has an amazing set of enzymes and colour guards that will render all your clothes whiter than white? Does this list of features connect with your emotional brain such that you want to buy my washing powder?

Storytelling often starts with the counterintuitive – defying expectation or challenging conventional thinking altogether. That was the wisdom behind one of Unilever's iconic brands when Persil was given the storytelling treatment in a campaign that has since won more effectiveness awards than any other. The creative team at Lowe and Partners tuned in to what mums have known all along – that children need the freedom to experience, develop and grow and that means getting dirty. The 'Dirt is good' campaign has defined the Persil brand ever since in more than 60 countries and the spin-off campaigns keep coming ten years later.

Storytelling in business?

We need more of it. Arguably, and strangely, it is the PR sector which is tasked with telling the story of businesses, that has been lagging behind in the use of storytelling. Take a look at the press centres on the websites of leading global brands that should know better. Still we see self-congratulating press releases about contract wins and strategic partnership agreements. New product launch press releases litter the digital ecosystem endlessly listing the features and benefits of the latest widget that the vendor is 'delighted to announce the launch of.' So what exactly is storytelling and how can it be applied to the process of promoting your business?

More importantly, how can storytelling influence sales? The ways in which businesses can harness the power of story go beyond the press release. The sales team on an exhibition stand, the CEO presenting to the board, the weekly staff meeting; all are situations where storytelling can inspire action. The great orators of history know that storytelling takes root in the emotional brain.

Movements are created when audiences are inspired – notably from Gandhi to Martin Luther-King to Winston Churchill. Great storytelling causes people to see and feel something in a way that a list of bullet points cannot.

The anatomy of a good story

We can learn a great deal from the author of a book or a scriptwriter of a play to understand how we can make our next campaign worthy. An author cannot take it for granted that you will keep turning the pages of their book unless you are emotionally engaged in the content. So the first element to the story design is having a plot. Professional storytellers, such as journalists, will tell you that good news doesn't sell. The same applies to the plot of a film or a book. So what does?

Bad news sells

Bad news is what drives the daily agenda of virtually every news headline. The plot of your story needs tension; a struggle, some kind of conflict at its heart. Your audience will relate better to a problem because it's the basic premise of gossip. So how do we apply this technique in practical terms when you simply have a widget to sell? Every invention ever created is designed to solve a problem. Find the fundamental problem your product or service solves and build a drama around it.

Let's take a plastic desk tidy – a small object that sits on the desk, holding pens and paper clips. The manufacturer will be tempted to list the features and benefits of their desk tidy and even give it a name. The company will tell you that you can order it in an array of bright colours. And it is made from long lasting durable plastic. It will hold as many as ten pens, paper clips and pieces of paper. And it's fire-proof. This is not storytelling.

Now let's look at the message through a different lens. A more imaginative way would be to create a drama caused by untidy desks (the problem). Could this be a story about poor productivity (unfolding drama) or can we spark curiosity by illustrating what an untidy desk may say about you? We could even show pictures of the desks of famous people with insights from a psychologist hired by the manufacturer. The creative possibilities are endless. If this were a press release then, what would it look like? 'Untidy desks to blame for poor productivity and competitiveness of business, according to Universal Plastics at the launch of its TidyBox range'... Better.

The human touch

Another technique favoured by the professional storyteller is to weave human interest into the plot. The audience will relate better to the story if it can identify with the characters or personalities. There is invariably a victim or a hero or both in a given plot of a book, so why not a press release? Again, our friends at Universal Plastics could take heed. Could we profile someone famous for being highly productive who always insists on having a tidy desk? Could that person bring a personal anecdote to the party that might back up the claim that poor productivity is the outcome of untidy desks? Can we refer to the great works of this famous person? A film director, or inventor, or scientist perhaps? If they are known for prolific output, the message could link nicely to the story.

Topical Timing is often a consideration

The audience may relate better to your story if there is a seasonal angle. Might the Universal Plastics product launch work better earlier in the New Year as office workers are returning to work and perhaps more open to different working practices at the start of a year than, say, in the summer? Is there such a thing as 'Office Tidy-up Day?' Could you create one if there isn't?

Story structure

Don't forget story structure. You need to be clear about this when thinking about stories for your business. The best approach you could take is to think of your business like a Pixar film. All Pixar films follow a very simple but hugely effective story structure.

Once upon a time there was _____. Every day _____. One day, _____. Because of that, _____. Because of that, _____. Until finally, _____.

Now think about your business and how you could tell your story using this approach. You will be amazed at how much more interesting your company can sound if you bring the drama that you solve alive in this way.

The best stories?

Let's come back to the Persil campaign and understand why it was so successful. It beautifully encapsulated all three dimensions in a single story. The 'bad news' or tension is dirt. It is there in your face. It contains all the drama in brutal simplicity, surprising an unsuspecting audience and grabbing attention in the process. The human interest is self-evident. Mums are the target audience and now they are an active participant in the story itself. Mums know dirt is good because they know their children are exploring, and that is healthy. As an observer, we can also see children at play. And that is good also. Topicality abounds in this story, because we want our children to put down their computer games and get active. This story plays superbly well in this context.

Undoubtedly, the best stories are the ones that feature all three dimensions but it also plays equally well in a b2b and b2c context. The anti-virus software company Kaspersky Lab in the UK once put out a compelling piece of content to coincide with Safer Internet Day by bringing all three elements into a single press release that went on to achieve widespread coverage in national press, lifestyle and broadcast media globally.

The PR team worked together to create a story that cost nothing to produce but the coffee and biscuits they shared. In the brainstorm, they identified how easy it would be for a young child watching Peppa Pig or Postman Pat on YouTube to find themselves watching inappropriate adult material. The answer was just three clicks. And so the headline was born.

The Three Clicks from Danger press release went on to be nominated for countless awards and was heralded as an example of best PR practice after achieving a global spread of more than 400 clippings across broadcast, online and in traditional print media. There is no question, every business could do with an injection of creative storytelling more often along these lines.

Brand storytelling

This approach obviously works when you are writing stories for the media about your business or creating campaigns that your sales team can use but can it be applied to brand? We have talked about humanising what you do but can you think of a brand as human? The answer to this question should be yes because your brand humanises your business as it demonstrates your values and personality.

Think about Apple. They make beautiful and brilliant computers but that isn't what their brand is about. Instead all of their advertising and public relations work is pointed in the direction of demonstrating their brand values and personality.

They don't run advertisement campaigns talking about how fast their computers are or what you can do with them. Instead they talk about wanting to change the world. They embrace change and applaud the people who bring it about. Their strap line of "Think Different" is a superb piece of brand storytelling and features throughout the business.

The same goes for Nike. They don't run campaigns talking about how cushioned their trainers soles are instead they celebrate the athletes who are pushing boundaries (using their trainers/products).

As an entrepreneur you need to think about your business as a human and identify what you want your brand to stand for. A brand is your promise – to you, your staff and customers. But if you're not authentic and consistent, your messaging will quickly fall on deaf ears. To win hearts and minds you need to be convincing.

Branding is about demonstrating your core value(s). If you know what you stand for you need to work hard to always deliver it. Everyone should be clear about what your core values are and when you hire new people they need to believe what you believe.

As Simon Sinek says "people don't buy what you do; they buy why you do it. If you talk about what you believe, you will attract those who believe what you believe.

Whether you're a legacy brand or a disruptor, the consistency of brand message across everything you do is everything – your brand is your differentiator. There's only one Apple, one Starbucks, one Nike. Many can copy or aspire to be these brands, but it's obvious and people generally don't buy into it as much or wholeheartedly. Why have second best when you can have the real deal?

Great storytelling is the game changer. It can make brands stand out and as Ian Rowden, CMO of the Virgin Group said: The best brands are built on great stories.

Stories drive action

Simon Sinek's 'Start with Why' philosophy (if you haven't read this book stop what you are doing and buy a copy now) is a great place to begin where the message is not what you do or how you do it differently. It is why you do it. Identify your cause, your belief, your passion and build a storytelling platform congruous with your brand strategy and messaging. Then make sure you can easily bridge from the story to the brand of product you are pushing. Only then will your story have the happy ending that every business wants. And what every business wants is more sales. Maybe we should call it storyselling.

So start by looking at your own brand now, or the brand you work for, and using Simon Sinek's Golden Circle theory, write down the answers to 'what, how and why' for your company but always start with why.

Think about the language you use. Every word counts, especially when it comes to your strapline and only make promises that you really mean and are prepared to keep.

A brand story is a cohesive narrative that encompasses the facts and feelings created by your brand. Unlike traditional advertising, which is about showing and telling about your brand, a story must inspire an emotional reaction.

Wrap up of tips for successful storytelling

Not every business sells items that are 'beautiful' must haves. Sometimes in business the things that sell are really mundane but you can sell anything with the right story, because people buy stories.

Remember the cornerstones of a compelling story:

- Bad news. Human interest. Relevant.
- Think in terms of LOTS (language of the senses) so the audience can see, feel, smell, even touch your story.
- In order to be a story, you need a plot with a tipping point, emotion, characters, a problem and a resolution.
- Think in graphical terms: show, not tell.
- Start with why?
- Be consistent
- Be authentic
- Be extraordinary.

Paul Stallard

About the author

Paul Stallard is the MD and investor in Berkeley Communications, a top ten tech PR agency in the UK. During his time working at Berkeley Communications he has overseen growth in the business, taking it from revenues of £900k to £4m. He has also led an acquisition of a German PR agency and now leads the team in Munich as the geschäftsführer.

Stallard has also founded and launched a full service research agency called Arlington Research and is aware of the many pitfalls of running businesses but also the many joys.

Outside of the day job he is a member of the Superbrand Council, a judge for the PR Week awards and previously for the PRCA and CIPR awards. A regular blogger, Stallard enjoys sharing his ideas and the examples of great work he has come across to the business community.

www.berkeleypr.com

www.paulstallard.com

www.arlingtonresearch.global

Outsourcing Made Simple

Susan Wilkin

Outsourcing has become increasingly popular over the last decade and most especially for entrepreneurs. Outsourcing allows a business owner to focus on building their business instead of being stuck with the day to day tasks that need to be completed. To help them do this, they have taken to looking for consultants, contractors and freelancers to take on these tasks. This is essentially a strategic solution for owners to grow a business without the need for a major investment of hiring staff members inhouse. Hiring staff members inhouse can be a large capital investment for any business and finding that right team member can be difficult.

There are two types of outsourcing available. The first type is outsourcing 'locally', which means to hire the services of people from outside a company but within the same country. The second type is to outsource 'offshore'. Offshore involves contracting service providers from other countries for a much cheaper cost. The most popular places for offshore providers are based in the Philippines or India.

Why you should outsource

Previously it used to be just big business that outsourced tasks to consultants and specialists but now the market is open to Solopreneurs, Entrepreneurs and small businesses. The main reason to outsource is to build your profits and to grow your business by working on the things only you can do. Essentially your specialist area. When you step away from the day-to-day operations and release yourself from having to oversee every piece of every project, you will have the time and energy to focus on business growth projects.

There are many reasons why a company may choose to outsource certain business functions. Some of the most common reasons include:

You feel overwhelmed: Many entrepreneurs like to do everything themselves especially in the early days. They feel exhausted by the long list of tasks that need to be completed and quite often overwhelmed.

You dislike the work: Entrepreneurs are good at what they do, but nobody is good at everything. If you have tasks that you simply dread doing or perhaps you always put them off until the last minute; this is a great indicator that you need to outsource this work.

It takes you forever to…. If you burn up many hours trying to draft your weekly newsletter because you struggle with the design, stop! It's not worth it when you can outsource the task, and have it completed quickly.

You don't know how to do something: If you've been doing without something because you can't do it yourself, outsourcing it to a specialist is the best answer. This means it will be completed quickly, efficiently and done correctly. Outsourcing offshore can gain access to a world-wide knowledgebase and some world class capabilities that may not be available in your own country.

Tasks are getting pushed aside: If emails and phone calls are going unanswered, then your customer service may be suffering. Poor customer service can lead to lost sales. Regardless of the task, if you do not have time to do it, hire someone to take care of it for you.

The family is unhappy: Take your queues from family and friends. When family members start migrating to your office, rather than you to the family room, chances are you're working too much and need more help.

You are tired of doing it alone: It's tough operating a one-person business. You have to be the creative thinker, implementer, follow-up person and more. While doing everything is great for the ego, it's not always great for business. Remember, even superheroes call in reinforcements when they need it.

Internal staff are struggling: Do you have other internal staff that are struggling to get through the workload? Outsourcing some of their tasks as well as your own will free up your staff's time, energy and focus to work on more important aspects of your business.

Expand and gain access to new areas: Delegating tasks to external freelancers means you can leverage and build in a buffer to increase internal profits. One of the smartest parts of outsourcing is to expand and gain access into new market areas, to be able to offer services that you couldn't offer before.

Increase Efficiency: Many freelancers are specialists in their areas, so you will be able to streamline or increase efficiency of those mundane and time-consuming functions

Quality Guarantee: Outsourcing firms usually have a guarantee for their services, whereas internal processes are not guaranteed unless you or someone in your team is overseeing them.

Harnessing operational best practice: You will have access to operational best practices that would be too difficult or time consuming to develop in-house.

Business Compliance: Being compliant in business can be difficult to navigate. Professional outsourcing firms that specialize in these and similar business areas keep pace with government regulations to ensure that you mitigate your risks.

Take that holiday: Leisure time is so important and as an entrepreneur there is always something to do in your business. By outsourcing work you can create a fantastic work/life balance which is probably one of the reasons you got into business in the first place. Take that holiday and enjoy your entrepreneurial lifestyle.

As you can see from the above, entrepreneurs that are overworked understand there are many reasons to outsource various tasks, but the biggest benefit seems to be the fact that it gives them access to expert or specialist help at a fraction of the cost.

What to outsource

A common question that is asked often is what to outsource. My advice is to always start small and grow big. One of the first things I outsourced was my house cleaning and lawnmowing which has over the years grown. In your business, here are some of the tasks that you can outsource.

- Graphic Design including image creation, logo design and a strategic consistent look for your business
- Marketing including strategy, list generation, social media, email and internet marketing
- Bookkeeping including invoicing payroll processing, credit control, accounts receivable and payable.
- Website Development, creation and maintenance including latest updates, shopping cart integration and developing a CRM

- General Administration/Virtual Assistant Services including transcription services, typing, data entry, replying to email enquiries, appointment setting and calendar management.
- Reception including telephone answering, appointment bookings, customer service, transferring calls and message taking
- Business Development including Sales Systems, strategies and customer service
- Customer relations management including customer follow up, surveys and managing a CRM database, sending proposals and quotations.
- SEO services for website optimisation, key word research and helping to get your website ranking to the top of search engines.
- Copywriting such as blog posts, website content, newsletters and content for brochures.
- Security services such as CCTV monitoring and 24-hour support.
- Recruitment services including recruitment of a freelancer, consultant or an internal staff member, they can conduct interviews, sort out resumes and find the right person for you.

This is not a full or complete list of the services that can be outsourced, there are many more. Ultimately, you know your business well and are in the *best* position to know what you can and want to outsource.

How do we outsource?

So now that we have an idea of what to outsource, the trick is to decide how to outsource. As I mentioned before there are two ways to outsource - either locally onshore or internationally offshore.

First off let's define some of the things you need to do in your business and are good at. These are normally the things that you wake up early in the morning and get started on straight away. They're the things that make your day to complete.

The next is the tasks you dislike or dread completing, or you are not good at. These are normally the tasks that you procrastinate on and they take you a very long time to do.

Next, write down some of the tasks you would like to delegate or could easily start to delegate to someone that was good at that task and enjoyed completing it.

What I need or want to do and what I am good at	Things that need to be completed that I am not good at or dread doing	What I can delegate

From this list, you should come up with at least 10 tasks that you can outsource right now. These will then need to be comprised into different categories of specialist services, mundane or repetitive tasks and highly skilled/expertise knowledge.

Highly Skilled or Expertise knowledge for example may be accountancy services or web developments.

Specialized Services relate to IT knowledge, computer or network setup or Marketing services

Repetitive / Everyday jobs relate to data entry, replying to emails, answering phones. They are similar each day.

From there you can organise the professionals you require to assist you with these tasks. To find the right professional can be difficult as each person or business comes with different attributes, skills and service offerings although they can offer similar services. This can make navigating the freelance world a bit of a nightmare.

Who to hire?

As a virtual assistant can be one of the first people you hire as part of your team, I thought I would focus on the hiring of a virtual assistant in this chapter as they can cover many of the tasks in your business.

No two virtual assistants are the same and they all come with a range of experience and expertise.

You already understand the type of specialisation you require for the types of tasks to be completed and you can break this down further especially if you will require more than one virtual assistant.

You can break them into Basic, Intermediate or Advanced experience. Then it is time to look at some of the traits that the virtual assistant should possess to fulfil your vision and current tasks.

Which are most important to you? Here are a few traits to get you started:

- **Can-Do Attitude.** The virtual assistant is not scared to jump in and give it a go.
- **Forward Thinker.** They see the whole picture and offer ideas and ways to implement tasks to help you reach your goals.

- **Self-Motivated.** They are proactive go-getters. They don't wait until the last minute to start a project.
- **Dependable.** They ensure work is completed as requested and delivered on time.
- **Trustworthy**. The virtual assistant is someone that you can build a relationship with and someone that is trusted.
- **Initiative**. If they see something that needs to be completed, they get it done without being asked.
- **Resourceful.** If they don't know the answer to something or how to do something, they know how to find it or learn it.
- **Organised.** Highly organised virtual assistants normally use project management tools such as Asana to stay organised and to also help you stay organised too.
- **Efficient**. Efficiency is a must in business and can be the difference between getting a sale or not.
- **Good Communicator.** Good communication reduces confusion and errors. When they can clearly see your vision and what you want competed, the virtual assistant can quickly get to work.
- **Professional.** They conduct themselves in a professional, self-confident way

While thinking about the traits for your virtual assistant, you may want to take it a step further and consider the type of personality it takes to do the job. For instance, if your virtual assistant will be talking to your customers, they'll need to be friendly and be great on the phone.

If they are sending emails and correspondence to your customers a great typing speed, attention to detail, along with being confident at writing correspondence is a must.

How to start working with a contractor

Next step is how to start working with the contractor/freelancer or virtual assistant:

Communicate with Your Virtual Assistant

The only way you will be confident and comfortable in working with a contractor is if you build a relationship with them. The first step to trusting someone with important details of your business is communicating with them. You can check their testimonials and even look through references to give you some background. Peace of mind comes with knowing more.

The most important part in maintaining a great working relationship with your contractor is to make communication a priority. You need to communicate your expectations clearly and leave no room for confusion, because this is the only way to get the best results. Schedule in meetings with your contractor, whether via telephone, Skype or face to face (depending on location).

Regular communication will ensure that you build a fantastic relationship with your contractor. It will also ensure that they become an extension of you and your business. By becoming an extension of your business, the contractor will be able to complete tasks with minimal supervision from yourself.

Understanding Your Business

Once you start working with your contractor it is important they understand your business. This means they need to completely understand how your business functions and how their tasks make an impact.

Hiring a person with experience in your industry is often preferred, however some induction notes will also help as well.

You can include the following in an induction pack for your contractor or they can compile this for you as one of their first tasks:

- A couple of paragraphs about your business
  - Who you are
  - What services or products you provide
  - Your target market
  - Office hours or times you prefer to work
  - Best contact numbers and times you can be reached for questions
- A couple of tasks to get the Virtual Assistant started
  - Include usernames and passwords
  - A basic procedure the virtual assistant can build upon
  - Any key phrases or terms you like to use in your correspondence
  - Scripting for phone calls
  - Deadline

Discuss About Compensation Upfront

Making payment arrangements upfront and sticking to them will ease a lot of tension in your working relationship with your contractor. You can choose to pay hourly or based on tasks completed, but just be sure to work out the details before you begin working together. Money has the ability to get in the way of your working relationship, so always make sure that you stick to your payment arrangement no matter what.

Paying Attention to Time

Many offshore contractors are working on a different time zone. Always be clear about the time and time zone that you would like the work completed by. It is always a good idea to verify they are able to respond during your normal business hours or as per the scope of the work required. This means you may have to work in a suitable time to both yourself and your team for meetings or questions to be answered.

Specialized outsourcing firms pride themselves on customer service and will be more than happy to assist you in your business needs and to your requirements (within reason of course). By starting with the steps above, you can be sure of a great relationship with your new team member.

Hidden Risks in Outsourcing

Mitigating risk is important in business and outsourcing can come with its own risks. I don't want to scare you away from outsourcing, as it is a valuable strategy for businesses, so I thought I would touch on some of the issues that can come up and how to resolve those issues or mitigate those risks in your business.

Clear Communication: Ensuring that you have clearly explained the task and that the person has a good handle on the instructions to complete the task. Using videos and written instructions with screen shots can be effective in ensuring the task is completed well.

Underquoting: Beware contractors that underquote. There can sometimes be hidden costs or when they get further into the contract and realise they have underquoted, they can demand more money to cover these costs.

Hourly Rate Explosion: Each contractor works at a different pace so contractors that work on an hourly rate can work at a slower pace than you expect or compared to another contractor. Always be clear with your expectations or estimates or ask for a time estimate.

Holidays: Many countries celebrate many different holidays throughout the year so when you are outsourcing to a different country be aware of their public holidays, sick leave requirements and also government practices for employment. Some countries do consider contractors to be employees so it is worth doing your research.

Many things must be done to outsource a business process: This can range from simple things such as moving files and ensuring the contractor has the available applications to complete the task and then progress checks to ensure that you are going to hit deadlines.

Is the outsourcing process always easy? No. You want a flexible and innovative partner who understands your business from the start, but this can only come with time or finding the right person. Sometimes you must trial a few contractors before you find the right fit for your company, someone you would like to work with long term.

In this chapter we have covered what outsourcing is, why you should, what you can, how you can and some of the issues that you can experience in outsourcing. As mentioned, outsourcing is a fantastic way to expand your business very quickly and then you can either hire staff members or scale with more contractors or team members. As an entrepreneur it is worth looking at the results that can be reaped from outsourcing and if you haven't started yet, then it is time to hire your first contractor.

Susan Wilkin

About the author

Susan Wilkin is a highly experienced Australian Virtual Assistant who has really taken her business to the next level. With her professional approach to her business and wealth of experience in the virtual assistant field, Susan brings to you, the business owner practical strategies that you can implement in your business today.

After delving into business as a virtual assistant in July 2009 offering very basic administration services, Susan's business Adminaholics has grown over the last 9 years to also include marketing, training, consulting, online courses and info-products to make it a viable business with different income streams.

Susan's expertise has been sought after by Authors, Trainers and Speakers who also specialise in different fields. Not only is Susan an innovative thinker but is known for achieving that end goal and next level results.

Susan is also a consultant with 121 Temps who coaches and trains many virtual assistants to build successful and viable businesses. Due to her wide scope of working with virtual assistants and other small businesses, Susan really understands the finer points of outsourcing.

8 Essential Public Speaking Skills Every Entrepreneur Needs For Business

Trish Springsteen

"If you can't communicate and talk to other people and get across your ideas, you're giving up your potential." Warren Buffett

In business every entrepreneur is looking for that special edge, the one that puts them in a more competitive position. Many entrepreneurs are focused on such topics as customer satisfaction, more effective procedures, marketing, leads and sales.

But I bet very few have considered improving the one thing that is at the core of all these problems. It is a simple fact that effective public speaking and communication skills are extremely good for business.
In business today, there is very little activity at any level which does not depend on good communication skills. Public speaking is the tip of the communication iceberg.

The skills that you learn as a public speaker:
- Know your audience

- Know your message – what you want to achieve, what you want the audience to take away

- The structure of your speech

- Attention catching openings

- Call to action conclusions

- Storytelling

- Connecting with the audience with eye contact, vocal variety and body language

- Ensuring there is a balance between information and emotional connection

All of these skills are the same skills you need to be an effective communicator to connect with your clients, your customers, your team, your staff, your peers and your suppliers.

Worried about customer satisfaction? Then having improved communication skills will have an immediate effect in this area. Frustrated that you have to spend so much time in repeating requests; re-stating statements and fixing up the results of miscommunication? Going into a boardroom to pitch your business? Just think how much more effective time you would have with improved personal communication skills.

And yet when considering what can be done to improve their position in the market, entrepreneurs rarely consider these skills and in fact very rarely include them as part of their business and marketing plans.

So what can you do to ensure that you are prepared in your business to succeed, to increase your leads, close sales, share your message, enhance your communication skills and have the confidence to grab opportunities?

"Sometimes all you need is 20 seconds of insane courage. Just literally 20 seconds of embarrassing bravery and I promise you something great will come of it." We Bought a Zoo, Benjamin Mee

First Step in the journey is to Overcome that Fear of Public Speaking. For most of us that fear is the fear of the unknown, fear of what the audience will say, fear of what our peers will think, fear that we may be found to be a fraud. This is that negative self-talk that says to us – you can't do that, you're not good enough. When you recognise that self-talk starting visualise a big red STOP sign. You don't want to go down that downward spiral of negativity. Stop right there. Get rid of the negativity and replace with positive talk. I am good enough, I am an expert, I have a message. Adopt a positive attitude. Believe in yourself and dismiss those quiet voices of doom and gloom and replace them with some strong positive affirmations.

Nerves are energy which manifests itself in the familiar symptoms of dry mouth, shaking hands, sweaty palms and all the rest of the debilitating feelings which makes it difficult for us to perform to our best ability.

We need to understand that the symptoms of performance anxiety and the symptoms of exciting anticipation are exactly the same; the only difference is in our attitude to the activity which causes them.

Remember to breathe! Breathe before you go into that important meeting with your client, breathe before you get up to speak at your first network meeting and breathe before you speak up and share your passion and message. Two or three deep breaths will centre you and give you the energy to make those first words count.

"You can speak well if your tongue can deliver the message of your heart."
John Ford

Second Step is to be Genuine. There is a lot of talk around about authenticity and it really is vitally important. People will work with those they like, know and trust. You cannot build that rapport with someone who is not genuine, who is not able to come out from behind that mask of uncertainty and step up and share their message. Let your passion shine when speaking about your business to clients, staff, or suppliers. Be you.

"We have been given two ears but a single mouth in order that we should hear more and talk less." Zeno of Citium ancient philosopher 2000 years ago

Third Step is Learn to Listen. Communication is a two way process, but if you start with focusing on your listening skills you will have a much better understanding of what people actually say to you. To understand your audience as a public speaker you need to focus on what they are after, are they with you on your speaking journey, do they understand your message?

People do not listen very well. They are more concerned with what they are going to say as soon as they can get a word in edgeways, than actually giving attention and interest to what is being received. Often we interchange the words "HEARING' and 'LISTENING' as if they meant the same thing, but of course they don't.

HEARING is thought to be passive – the act of receiving the sound through the ear. We can often hear things without being really conscious of it. The early morning bird chorus can be heard, but to identify one bird song we need to actively listen.

LISTENING involves a conscious effort to understand what is being said. Listening means that we try to make sense of what we have heard. Active listening requires concentration not for the sound but for the meaning. Become a listener and concentrate on what is being said without judgement or bias.

And if you do not understand something take the time to clarify it. A simple question such as "I am not sure I understand what you meant, can you explain it again to me." will allow the speaker to rephrase it.

When you have listened, you are in a better position to undertake clear communication yourself.

Listening plays a vital part in customer/client service and dealing with difficult clients. Listen for the facts not the emotion. Listen to what the client is saying beneath the emotion. Be objective and be aware that, in the main the client is annoyed at the situation, not with you personally. Unless you have erred. In which case acknowledge the error fix it and move on. If you can be objective and not let your emotions become engaged then you will find it easier to deal with an emotional client.

In many cases just listening and acknowledging the issues will defuse most difficult clients. Validating a client's issues will often be enough.

"Before we even sit down to work on our presentation we need to be absolutely clear what we need to achieve. We need to fully understand the purpose of the presentation." Trish Springsteen: Creating Confident Communicators

Fourth Step: Organise Your Thoughts. To be able to be understood you need to have a clear outline of what you are speaking about. We think very much faster than we speak, so taking a few moments out to organise what we want to say will not impact on our communication, it will improve it.
We need to know quite clearly in our own mind what our main aim is going to be. If we are not clear on this our communication is going to be erratic, unfocused and ineffective. We should ask ourselves what do I want this person to know or to do?

You need to be very focussed on what your goal is, what outcome you want to achieve with this audience, at this point of time and in the time allowed. If you are not clear on your destination and how you want to reach it; how can you take your audience or your client along with you?
This is the key to clear and effective communication.

"It usually takes me three weeks to prepare a good impromptu speech." Mark Twain

Fifth Step: Impromptu Speaking. Unfortunately we don't have three weeks to prepare our impromptu responses. Questions often come out of the left field. Usually at meetings, someone will turn to you and say "And what do you think of the idea?" Why is that we can't think of anything to say until at least two hours after the meeting.

How can we manage to respond competently to an abruptly posed question that we don't have three weeks to prepare for?

If you have a meeting ask yourself "What is on the agenda? Is there anything that applies to my position or my department? Are there any controversial issues which I may be asked to comment on?" Make sure that you have your answers with you.

If you are going into a media interview, think about the questions you may be asked. What are the issues? What was the media release about? What part of your business could be related to the latest trending issues?

So you have made some preparations, but how can you structure the response so you sound in control, competent and make it clear and concise?

Before you really start to work at your response you need to make sure that you really understand the question. So:

Listen to the question carefully. Many people actually only listen to the first five to ten seconds of the question before they start working on the response. This can mean that you answer the question you thought you heard rather than the question which was asked. So listen all the way through before anything else.

Next, ask yourself "What do I know about that? If the topic is completely unknown to you just admit it. If it is something that you need to obtain further information on, then say so.

However, if you know the answer that is what you focus on when constructing a reply. Use this very simple formula to remain focused:

P   is for the Point – This is the answer to the question. It is the WHAT and shows that you know what you are talking about. You're informative.

R   The Reason for the point –. It is the WHY and shows that you know what you are talking about. It could be a simple explanation, or background information which helps to make your Point clear and helps to show that you are a credible source of information.

E   The Examples/Explanation of points – Personal examples can help you make your point clear. When you can cite personal experiences to demonstrate your point of view, you become a believable source.

P   Restate your Purpose for Speaking – this is a brief recap, which rounds the response off and gives your listeners a clear indication that you have finished your reply. You have responded concisely.

Then STOP speaking. You have finished your answer.

This simple formula is the basis for most information communication and presentations. It explains in straightforward terms what you know. You make your information relevant with good reasons before making it personal. Finally, restating the purpose of speaking again signals to your listeners that you have completed your response.

This time, when driving home instead of going over what you should have said, you can bask in the achievement of what you did say.

"There are four ways, and only four ways, in which we have contact with the world. We are evaluated and classified by these four contacts: what we do, how we look, what we say, and how we say it." Dale Carnegie

Sixth Step: Watch the Body Language. While you are speaking watch your listeners for feedback. You may notice that they are looking confused.

Stop! You may need to rephrase the statement, or restate the information in another way. You might find that your listeners clearly do not agree with what you are saying, and you have the opportunity to allow them to voice their opinions. Being able to address concerns immediately usually has a very positive effect on your listeners.

You will also be able to see the nod, the smile and the positive body language which will indicate that you have agreement. This applies when presenting to groups or with individual clients. Be very aware of the non-verbal indications, not only of your audience or client, but also of the non-verbal vibes that you are giving off. Your verbal message must be congruent with the non-verbal or you will have mixed results. Your clients and your audiences will more often believe the non-verbal over the verbal if they are faced with a mixed message.

"Stop thinking of 'video marketing' as this separate entity that is optional for your business. Video is an effective form of communication that needs to be integrated into each and every aspect of your existing marketing efforts." James Wedmore

Seventh Step: Get Comfortable With Videos. Videos allow you to personally share your message and business. Your clients can see who you are and what you are passionate about. Expand your speaking skills and step outside your comfort zone. A good place to start could be by giving a video testimonial to someone you have worked with, bought from, attended their workshop, or done business with.

Video testimonials are a golden opportunity for you to advertise your own business whilst saying something nice and worthwhile about the workshop you have attended or person you have done business with. Testimonials are a marketing opportunity for you – use it, don't waste it.

Follow these simple guidelines and you will be on your journey to making videos work for you and your business.

1.   Step forward and say YES

2.   Give yourself a few minutes to structure in your mind what you are going to say. If you are really proactive you will already have thought this through and have realised how you can utilise your speaking skills and are using them.

3.   Speak Clearly and don't rush – use pause to highlight the points you are sharing

4.   Look straight at the video and speak as if you are speaking to a friend sharing the wonderful time you have just had

5.   Start with your name and your business

6.   Give one or two constructive thoughts on the workshop or event – make it meaningful and quantitative if possible. Just saying it was great, is not enough. If you can pick one or two points that will change or enhance your business it will be more valuable to the presenter and will ensure that your testimonial is used. Work on sharing the benefits you have gained from the event.

7.   Keep it concise

8.   Finish with your name and your business

Work on becoming comfortable with videos. Giving video testimonials allows you to get used to appearing in front of the camera. The next step is to see where you can use your speaking skills to incorporate videos into your business.

They could be on your website, Facebook posts, in your blogs, on LinkedIn, on YouTube or as part of an online course. The possibilities are endless as you enhance your public speaking skills and confidence.

"Most people are more deeply influenced by one clear, vivid, personal example than by an abundance of statistical data." Elliot Aronson

Eighth Step: The Power of Storytelling.

As human beings we are almost conditioned to respond to stories. They are part of our culture. From early times our history and our laws were passed down through stories. The story teller was an important person in the tribe.

As a public speaker stories are used to connect with the audience. Stories allow the speaker to showcase teaching points, share a message, and show their genuine side to the audience.

In the same way the entrepreneur can use stories to connect with the client. The stories can be about the wins other clients have had. They can showcase the journey the clients have taken with you and how you have helped them to overcome their pain, their issues and their problems.

You can share your story with your clients so that they can build on the like, knowing and trust. When a client can connect with you through your story and see that you know what you are talking about, that you have been there and gone through the same journey; then they are more likely to want to do business with.

So polish up your story telling skills – work on the word picture, the structure and your presentation. However, remember to ensure that the story is relevant to your message, your passion, your service and/or your product.

"Strength of your capability is tested in competition. Be bold, fearless and put forth your best to extract success. In the meantime, make sure that success is not the only accomplishment but also how you inspire others and project yourself as role model." Dr Anil Kumar Sinha

Bonus: A step most entrepreneurs miss in business is nominating for Business Awards. Business awards can be a valuable component in establishing your credibility and for your clients in recognising your expertise.

The public speaking skills outlined here will also be valuable in applying for these awards and of course will be immensely valuable when it comes time for your acceptance speech. And especially of value when you leverage your award win and start speaking to the media – print journalist, radio interviews and TV interviews.

"If the best real estate is all about 'location, location, location', then the mantra for running the best business has got to be 'communication, communication, communication'." Richard Branson

Incorporating all or some of these skills in your business will take you a long way on your journey to being an effective communicator and speaker. Transferring these public speaking skills and incorporating them into your entrepreneurial skills will ensure that you will never miss opportunities for your business or for yourself.

Trish Springsteen

About the author

Trish is the co-founder and owner of Trischel, a company dedicated to bringing communication and effective speaking skills to individuals, businesses and organisations.

An award winning trainer, mentor and author, Trish has spoken on national and international stages and she is passionate about creating confident communicators.

Having personally experienced the fear of public speaking and being lost for words when facing questions, and missing opportunities because of this, Trish is passionate about helping others conquer their fear of speaking and communication.

Trish has brought improved speaking and communication skills to published authors, bloggers and introverts. As well as communication, speaking and presentation skills to accountants from Crosbie Warren

Sinclair; executives from The IQ Business Group and Aurecon; scientists from Rio Tinto Alcon;
engineers from James Hardy and property retail experts from Jones Lang LaSalle.

In addition to be awarded the National Edupreneur 2015 Award in the Professional Speaking Category, Trish was also a Finalist in the ILAB Global Impact 2015 Awards and has been nominated for the Telstra Business Awards. Trish also has been awarded Toastmasters International Excellence in Marketing and Excellence in Education and Training Awards.

Trish is the author of:

Creating Confident Communicators

co-author of:

- Learning Can Be fun: Trischel's Book of Blogs

- A-Z of Interview Skills – How to Shine at Your Interview

And contributing author in

- Motivational Speakers Australia

- Picture Them Naked – Everything You Wanted to Know About Presenting and Public Speaking; and

- The Book of Success a life-changing book that offers precious, practical and thought-provoking insights that will inspire you to be the best you can be at home, at work, and everywhere in between.

Most importantly Trish loves what she does and she is having fun doing it.
Award   Winning   Public   Speaking   Mentor,   Coach,   Author
http://www.trischel.com.au http://www.trishspringsteen.com
Email: info@trischel.com.au

Strategies For Getting Ahead Using The Law Of Attraction

Nerida Mills

There I was, sitting in my car, the sun shining through the window as the car became hotter and hotter. I could hear the sounds outside. The cars driving by, the ships sailing past as they passed the docks and I just sat there with the biggest grin on my face in total amazement. It had worked!

It wasn't the first time I had used the law of attraction, but boy did it have obstacles to pass through to make this experience my reality.

I had started my business one year earlier after recently moving to Perth WA from Northern NSW. I had been living on 100 acres for the past 3 years with a group of people trying to form an intentional community. The community, or the "Luminous Heart Center" was a dream of the community members individually and we had come together with our common dream to create a place of healing for ourselves and others.

Three years in however and things weren't going according to plan. We had started in tents and over 6 months built a shed, children in tow. We had been washed out by torrential rains more times than I care to remember. We had set up fences and adopted an array of farm animals to help us maintain the land and sustain our life. We had planted fruit trees and veggie patches, built a community and planned a future. We had designed an eco village from our dreams. And then the dream had turned into a nightmare as it all came crumbling down.

I was pregnant at the time and ready to give birth in a matter of weeks when my family decided that the best chance we had to keep that dream alive was to get some space. We moved to WA with the intention on going back once things settled down somewhat.

After giving birth and a few months had passed I realised that going back was not an option and so moving forward became my drive. I explored my passions and was determined to find a way forward that was going to make my perceived loss "worth it". If I didn't get to live that, then what I would live would be mind blowing.

I sent myself into a whirlwind of the coaching world and human behaviour. Learning everything I could about how we create reality and what strategies I could adopt to ensure that the "failure" of the property would never be repeated. I was driven by a fear of experiencing that pain again.
Where did I go wrong? I would ask. We had used the law of attraction to acquire the property in the first place. This feeling that I had missed something in the process we used kept nagging at me. Why had it not worked? And how could I ensure that my life moving forward would not suffer the same fate? Human behaviour became my hope.

With the promise of 6 figure incomes and a future where I could rebuild my dream I set to the task of creating a training business based on the principles of Neuro linguistic programming and human behaviour.

It didn't take long for the feeling of 'fish out of water' to seep through the fear pushing me forward and for me to realise that I was going to need to give this everything I had. Not just the law of attraction I had known, not just the NLP principles to success but everything and then some that I had yet to discover...

I started by creating the space, and then the vision. A business space that I could run a 6 figure income business from. We had no money at the time so I got filing cabinets from hard rubbish, bought a cheap second hand desk and I was gifted a printer from my mum. I made a gratitude board, set my intention and stuck it up. I began a ritual of visualisation every morning before starting work. I would see myself shaking hands after signing a contract with a corporate organisation. I saw myself walking out of a building feeling amazed and elated and excited and grateful and proud.

I got help. Outside of getting the help I needed with the kids, I also employed a woman to teach me about marketing as I had no idea what I was doing. I was "a dirty hippy on the hill" this was going to take some rewiring!

And I got to work. Cold calling, offering free workshops to anyone who would have me, networking like a crazed person, meeting anyone and everyone within the business community.

It was about this time that my partner hurt his arm at work and was unable to go to work. We took it as a sign that it was the right thing to put everything I had into this business and I went full time. An act that required me to leave my 6 month old with his dad and with other carers, something I had never done with his older sisters and something that tore at my heart but I saw as necessary.

As I continued aiming for the stars my partner became more and more unsettled and unhappy. He began experiencing severe anxiety attacks around the same time as I gained my first clients. I needed to up my game. Take the pressure off, help give him the space to heal from all he had experienced in the breakdown of the community and the fallout from it all.

I wrote the new beliefs I needed to adopt on the mirror and would say them to myself every day. I continued my strategies in business and was gaining momentum. I had created a system of "bread and butter". My clients were covering my costs. I could hear the internal sigh of relief.

I had even gained some opportunities of corporate training, giving presentations to the likes of Telstra, in which I nailed the delivery and then freaked out at the sales pitch. No conversion.

I also started becoming obsessed with workplace culture and met a woman who held the same passion. We decided to go into a business together to bring workplace culture to Perth on a scale of some of the worlds leaders. We devoted all our time into creating the program and how we would deliver it. All the while my partner was becoming more and more destructive as he battled his own demons.

I was now reading my positive affirmations as I left the house, in the car at the lights. Anywhere to change the state I was in at home to one I could deliver the business I wanted to, to the world. We were fighting, a lot.

I was so determined that I could make my relationship better, I could make him better through making the business succeed. So I would ignore things, I would yell and scream and then get in the car and use everything I had learnt to change my state.

I was listening to audio book after audiobook on my travels to meetings, networking events and speaking gigs.

Then just weeks before the launch of the new venture, my business partner pulled out. Afraid of the instability I had at home.

There was a void. A point where I felt I was in a hole. I looked around at what I had done with my business and I realised I had dropped the ball on my bread and butter. I had no income in sight and I had turned my back on what I had established for the promise of even more. My partner lashed out, destroying my office as his internal pain was externalised and I was the target. I didn't know what to do. I was lost. Everything I had worked for over the past 10 months was in ruin and I was afraid.

I called my mentor unsure of how to move forward. I told her everything. Of how I had failed, of how I was scared, of how I thought I might have to give up. Silence. And then a whisper left my mouth, "but I really don't want to."

She offered to wipe some of the debt I owed her or to pay for some flights to attend a weekend workshop with her on the Gold Coast. I needed a break. I needed to refresh my spirits and I wasn't ready to give up yet. So I packed my bags and set off.

I came home with renewed focus, drive and motivation. I was going to work with women and help empower more women into leadership roles. The Shining Sistas workshop was created.

I launched this workshop as a lead in to work with me one on one. I delivered my first one just 2 weeks later to a sold out room and got amazing feedback. More than that though, I had delivered it to a woman unknowingly who worked in the corporate world. She worked in HR, and could see the potential in bringing this process to her workplace.

She organised a meeting with me and her boss to discuss and see if we would be able to work together. The meeting date was set.

A day before the meeting was to take place I left my partner. Our home life had become so destructive that I no longer felt safe in the home and would not have my children raised in that environment. So I left. My heart aching, tears in my eyes I arrived at my sisters. The few people I spoke to that day all said the same thing, reschedule the meeting. "You're in no state" They were right. I was in a terrible state and the old me that had attracted the property would have rescheduled. I would have taken it as a sign. "The time is not right."

But I was no longer that person and I knew that 99% of this game is showing up. I was in no state and perhaps that was for the best. I had nothing to lose. In the last 18 months I had moved away from my perceived dream at the time, lost one of my best friends to a car accident, given birth, started a business and now my relationship was over. I was going to tell this HR director exactly what I thought about women and women's leadership, let's face it, it probably wouldn't be a bad thing if I didn't get it. I had a lot to process.

So the next day I showed up in borrowed clothes and laid it all on the line.

"I love your passion and what you'd like to do with our ladies, can you put together a proposition?" "Sure" I said.

The next week was spent creating a framework for something I could deliver that would knock their socks off. I got a lot of advice and had well trusted people read and give feedback on the proposal and the price. Again I had no idea what I was doing, this was the first time I had been asked to put together anything for the corporate world and so that all too familiar feeling of fish out of water reminded me I was in new territory.

I doubled my price after some well-educated advice and sent it through.

I wanted this. And I knew I couldn't need it. Nothing kills abundance like desperation. And so I walked the thin line between desire and surrender.

Two weeks later I had my answer.

"Yes we want to go ahead but can we add 2 more women and round it off to $40,000?"

"I think that could work" was all I could stumble out as my hands shook and my body began to sweat knowing full well that I had never earnt that in a year, let alone 3 months.

We set the time to sign the contract and then, there I sat. Smile on my face. In total amazement. I had signed the contract and was sure to shake the woman and man's hands. I was amazed and elated and excited and grateful and proud.

And completely freaked out! Now I had to deliver!

This experience taught me many things and I now get to teach these things to other social conscious entrepreneurs. I now work with men and women all over the world who feel frustrated, unfulfilled and stuck to create the lifestyle and legacy they desire that will bring them passion, freedom and contribution, and I do that using this beautiful system based on everything I learnt and continue to implement myself.

1. Re-invent

Vision - Be bold with what you want to create.

With a focus on gratitude create a vision. Be specific, use a time frame and notice not only what you are doing and having but what you are feeling. This can be materialised through a gratitude board or goal book. Then bring this vision to life with daily visualisations. Again being specific and focusing on one thing at a time.

Plan - Now you know what you want, create the plan on how to get there. Reverse engineer this vision. What steps and at what times do you need to have completed these steps in order to reach your big vision? You can work this for 10, 5, 3 and 1 year plans. Break them down into your next 90 days, then 1 month and finally this week.

Act - Now that you know where you are heading and what you need to do to get there, take action! Work based on your weekly to do lists, ensuring to check back in with your bigger goals weekly and monthly. Ensure you embody behavioural flexibility, remember, sometimes things come to us in ways that were way outside of how we saw it, so be open.

2. Reawaken

Educate - Understand how you create your reality. Know that the world is full of possibility and potential that we can experience anything when we focus our attention and intention into the fully manifest experience of having that thing. Your world is currently made up by your beliefs, your values, your standards, your physiological state, the quality of your social space, what you surround yourself in or your environment and your personal frequency which is affected by everything else mentioned.

Reflect - Now that you understand how things work, understand how YOU work. Dive deeply into how you have created your experience and the things that may be blocking the experience you are trying to create. Be willing to be raw and honest with yourself and flexible enough to change in the ways you must. Grow as you grow.

Project - Use your environment to gage how you are going, where there is still growth, what areas need tweaking. And then tweak.

3. Re-connect

Align - yourself with who you want to be. Research people who have achieved what you want and learn how. What did they do? What did they believe? How did they hold themselves? What rituals did they employ? And then model them. Tweak your actions, strategies and behaviours to bring you more inline with the outcome you are looking to achieve.

Recreate your values, beliefs and standards consciously.

Let go - Evolve consciously who you think you are. Let go of who you used to be. That person created the results you have had in the past. It will take a new version of yourself to create what you want. Bravely and courageously jump off the metaphorical cliff.

Breakthrough - Step into who you are becoming. Be the person who has the experience. Implement all of what you have learnt and fully embrace the potential of this new you.

Here's what I know for sure:
We are greater than we could ever imagine.
Life, the universe, God, whatever, is ready and waiting to support, you, to fill you with joy and to be your unfolding.
When we follow our passion, our desire, what juices us up, life gets turned on!
You have everything you need within you right now. Your curiosity, essence, intelligence, determination, skill. It will take you where you need to be.
You will attract what you are, not what you want. Become what you want and you will experience it. If you want abundance, be abundant. If you want success be a successful business owner. (do what they do) If you want time, be time conscious.

Finally, how you do anything is how you do everything! Small things matter. Shift the small and the large will follow.

Nerida Mills

About the author

Nerida Mills is a transformational coach, NLP practitioner, hypnotherapist and psychosomatic therapist. All of these have one thing in common, they create sustained and ecological change in people in order for them to perform at their best, know themselves more truly and live life from a place of wonder and love.

Nerida is wildly curious about how we create experience and spends her time deepening her understanding in the field, developing her skills, helping her clients and home schooling her three young children.

She works with people in a variety of mediums, if you'd like to know more, check out her website at www.neridamills.com .

The Golden Keys of Networking

Tara Geraghty

Networking.

A single three-syllable-word that has the ability to conjure up all sorts of images, feelings, and fears in the minds of otherwise stable, successful adults. What should seem so simple sends most of us into paralysis. Working on the perfect "pitch" or catchy introduction has become an art entire books are dedicated to. Since many networking groups include a one minute introduction, and the fear of public speaking ranking higher than the fear of death, it's easy to see why networking is often met with a love/hate relationship.

Years ago networking was something reserved for conferences, trade shows, and alumni groups. Now with the boom of entrepreneurship, home-based businesses and the emergence of social media, networking happens every hour, every day, in every town. Simply scan Facebook, Meetup, or Eventbright and a multitude of opportunities will jump off the screen at you. The goal now becomes a matter of sifting through countless events to find the right one, the magic one: the one that will connect you with just the right people, at just the right time, who will go clamoring for your products and services.

Everyone from new business owners to college students are told:

"It's not what you know, it's who you know."

"The opposite of networking is NOT-working."

"Your network is your net-worth."

We even tell our children, *"A stranger is just a friend you haven't met yet!"*

Yet, if it's that simple, how come so many people struggle with it? Somehow, once it's labeled "networking" something that should be natural becomes stiff, awkward and canned. Even worse, most people are never actually taught *how* to network. They simply throw themselves into a networking event with blind faith thinking, *"This is what it takes to become successful and I'm willing to do whatever it takes!"* As a result, networking often looks like business cards thrown on a table, name tags with a title written under a name, and a classic formal handshake. If you've ever ventured out to a networking event maybe you have met one (or more!) of the following people:

Carl-the-Card-Thrower

> We all know him. He's the guy who walks around the room with his ultimate goal to hand out as many business cards as he can. He lives by the motto: I already know my name and phone number so I don't need my card, everyone else does. Going home with an empty business card case is his ultimate measure of success.

Ken-the-Card-Collector

> Like Carl, Ken is focused on numbers not actual networking. He collects just as many cards as he hands out. Unlike Carl, he understands, "the fortune is in the follow up," so giving out his card is not the goal. Building his contact list is. The more cards he goes home with the more people he can add to his list to send out spammy emails on a regular basis.

Sally Shy-ster

Sally forces herself to go to networking events because she really, *really*, wants to be successful. She keeps hearing networking is the key to success so she works up her courage to attend a minimum of two networking events each week. She often stands on the side lines, hoping someone will come up and talk to her but secretly terrified if they do because she has no idea what she will say. Small talk is her kryptonite. Normally she makes friends easily, but once that name tag goes on she finds herself stumbling over her words and engaged in long awkward pauses. She measures her success simply on the fact she stepped out of her comfort zone and showed up.

Dan-Drinks-a-Lot

Dan loves after hours networking. He loves to be the life of the party and as a single guy networking combines many of his favorite activities: happy hour, business and the potential of meeting an attractive woman. Never sure if he's approaching them about business or to comment on their legs women who have met him try to steer clear of him at events. As the event goes on, he usually gets louder and more boisterous. It's hard for anyone to take him seriously in business but everyone seems to refer to him as, *"The Man!"*

Tammy-Talk-a-Lot

> Tammy loves people. Networking is second nature to her. She easily approaches people and loves to tell them all about her business or product. By the end of the night she probably has talked to everyone, told them everything about her business, why her product is superior to every other company, and has a handful of cards from people who she knows nothing about, after all, she was the one doing all the talking.

While these examples may seem extreme it shows the ineffective and often confused approaches to networking. The problem stems from a simple misunderstanding of what networking truly is. Once we understand what authentic, genuine, *effective* networking is, anyone can learn to become a master networker. So let's first look at what networking is not.

Networking is not just:

- *Handing out business cards*
- *Collecting business cards*
- *Finding people to buy your product or services*
- *Selling*
- *Putting down your competition*
- *Meeting a ton of people*

So if that's what networking is *not*, then what exactly *is* networking?

According to **www.yourdictionary.com** networking is defined as:

> *"The act of making contact and exchanging information with other people, groups and institutions to develop mutually beneficial*

relationships, or to access and share information between computers."

Okay, we aren't computers so we don't need to worry about that, but let's go back to that first part. The act of making contacts and exchanging information to develop **mutually beneficial relationships**.

Mutually beneficial. How many of us approach networking that way? When we are speaking with someone are we thinking just as much about how we can help *them* as we hope they can help us? Now, I'm not talking about the person who is thinking, well of course I can help them, my product helps everyone! I'm talking about genuine, authentic, other's focused relationship building.

I'm about to share with you my five Golden Keys of networking. The five principles that if you incorporate into your networking will take you from, *"Hello my name is…"* to, *"Thanks, I appreciate your business!"* Are you ready?

The Golden Keys of Networking:

Golden Key Number One:

People like to do business with people that they like, and people like people who take a sincere interest in them and/or they have something in common with.

People like to do business with people they like. Okay, that seems easy enough, but how do we get people to like us? Let's start with thinking about the people *you* like. Why do you like them? Usually, because they make us feel important. They take an interest in us. They listen when we speak, respect our thoughts, feelings and opinions. They *care*. Make a list of the five people in your life you like the best. (Your family doesn't count.)

Why do you like them? How do you feel around them? What do they *do* that makes you feel this way? Next, start to ask yourself, "How can I make other people feel this way?"

This goes to point number two. People like people who take a sincere interest in them. The only way to do that is to ask questions. In authentic networking, we want to learn more about *them* then just tell them about us. If we are truly looking to find a need and fill it, we can only do that when we know enough about a person to determine if there even *is* a need. If you own a child care facility and I don't have a child, I don't have a need you can fill. I might be a connector for you but I am not your ideal client, and that's okay.

Finally, people like people they have something in common with. I learned this living in Denver as a born-and-bred bred Jersey girl. As soon as I would meet someone who was from the Tri-State area it was like an instant bond. We would commiserate over the lack of great Italian food, pizza and bagels. Joke about how everyone drove to slow and thought we talked too fast. It was instant friendship! What's the easiest way to find something in common with someone? Ask questions! Asking questions also takes the pressure off of us. We don't need to worry about what to say because the other person is the one who is doing all of the talking. Maybe you are both single mothers, share the same favorite sports team, both grew up out of state, both love the beach etc. It doesn't really matter...you're simply looking for common ground.

So that leads us to.....

How do you start a conversation? You only need to learn one thing: how to give a sincere compliment. Yup, that's it. It's my secret conversation starter. I find something to compliment them on or something we have in common and then ask, *"So what do you do?"* That's it. Really it *is* that simple.

Some examples:

"I love that necklace it's beautiful. So what do you do?"
"I noticed you talking to Brad, we met at this event last month. So what do you do?"
"Great shoes! So what do you do?"
"I noticed you seem to know everyone here, so what do you do?"
"Ah a fellow Budweiser drinker, cheers! So what do you do?"

This isn't rocket science. Remember, at a networking event everyone is there to ….network. They *want* to tell you what they do. They *want* someone to talk to as much as you want someone to talk to. Even better, they are usually relieved someone approached them!

Golden Key Number Two:

Don't ever underestimate your image.

According to www.businessinsider.com it takes only seven seconds to make a first impression. Seven *seconds*! That means when it comes to image, we cannot underestimate the value it has in our first impression. Why is image important when it comes to relationship building? Because no one is going to take the time to build a relationship with you if you don't look like someone they want to get to know, and in business, image counts. I remember years ago I used to run a networking luncheon for women in business. We would invite women to our studio for lunchtime makeovers and a chance to network with each other.

I was often shocked how women would show up to represent their business. Sneakers and jeans were not uncommon. Now, if you own a local garage shop you don't necessarily need to show up in a three piece suit, but you do want to look professional. Do you look like someone I would trust with my business? Is your business card clean and crisp or did you dig it out of your pocket and all four sides are slightly worn? Is the pen you used to jot my number down with chewed off on the end? Shoes polished? Nails well kept? Do you look like a successful business owner? Keep in mind, going out to happy hour to meet friends or a potential date is a different look than a happy hour networking event where you want to been seen as a successful business owner. One fabulous outfit that makes you feel like a million bucks is all you need. If you're not sure if your image is up to date ask a friend whose image you admire or consult with an image consultant. Some department stores even offer free image consultations when you shop there. A good rule of thumb is simply look in the mirror; would you seek out you at a networking event?

Golden Key Number Three:

Selling is finding a need and filling it, but you only know someone's need if you take the time to get to know them. Beware though, people will see through fake flattery, self-serving interest, and insincere small talk faster than you can say, "Hello, my name is...".

You cannot fake sincerity. Don't even try it. If you genuinely don't like people, or see people as a means to your personal end, you might as well change careers now. In the short term you might find some quick success but long term, repeat business will evade you and you will always wonder why. People feel our energy.

If our words don't match our true intent, people may not be able to verbalize what they feel, but they will instinctively avoid us. As Emerson said, *"What we are speaks louder than what we say."* When it comes to networking, remember you are looking for mutually beneficial relationships. This is all about go-give not go-get.

Golden Key Number Four:

Every person you meet knows an average of 500 people.

Don't think you know 500 people? Check out your Facebook friends list, your Instagram profile or even your cell phone. You likely have hundreds of contacts. And guess what? So does everyone else you meet. It's not necessarily the person you meet that will do business with you; it's the 500 people *they know* that just might. Referrals are often an overlooked but highly impactful piece of networking. And people refer... people they like! Think about who you're likely to refer yourself. Imagine your friend says they are thinking of buying their first home and asks if you know a great realtor. Now, of course, the best referrals are from people who have personally done business with us, but what if you don't have a realtor you have personally used? Your next thought is going to be the people you know who are realtors. You might know a handful of different realtors in your community, but who will you choose to refer? Probably the one you like the most!

Imagine this scenario: you know two realtors from your local networking group. One has been in business longer and has a more extensive portfolio for sure, but you just really *like* the other. The latter has taken the time to talk with you and learn more about your business, and has made an effort to remember your name and even introduce you to some of the other people in the group. I would venture to say, when it comes down to it, most of us will refer the slightly greener realtor who we really like, over the successful veteran whom we don't really care for. Credentials will only get you so far when it comes to networking. It's our personal relationships that will always have the last word when it comes to referrals.

So how do you get those great referrals? You must ask. The more specific you are, the easier it is for someone to think of a referral for you. For example, if you sell a weight loss product and ask me, *"Who do you know who needs to lose weight?"* I can probably think of five people right off the bat, but most of them I wouldn't refer because I wouldn't want to offend them! Now imagine if you asked, *"Who do you know that just had a baby and is looking to lose that extra baby weight?"* I might have just one person who pops into my mind but could easily refer you to. Get the idea?

I have worked in the skin care and cosmetic industry for 20+ years. Since everyone has skin *technically* anyone could be my client. Now imagine during my one minute introduction I say something like, *"A good referral for me is anyone with skin."* Can't you just picture the room of blank stares! However, when I ask for specific referrals people are more willing to connect me with the people I'm looking to meet. For example I might say, *"A good referral for me is someone who is getting married and starting to think about their wedding day makeup,"* or *"Who do you know that has a teenager with acne and might appreciate samples of our new acne line?"* See the difference?   Remember, when you feel like you don't know enough people think of each person you *do know* as a connector to 100, 200, or 500 + people! You do know enough people. You just need to continue to build the relationships you do have so others want to refer you. Which leads us to .....

Golden Key Number Five:

Relationships take time, effort, and do not happen at one event.

This is probably the second most misunderstood piece of networking (after the mutually beneficial piece!) Because I have had the privilege of facilitating numerous networking groups I'm sad to say I have seen this happen over and over. A new person will show up at an event for the first time. Sometimes they stay through the event or sometimes they might even leave early if they don't think there is anyone there they can "sell" to that day. They go home without a new appointment booked, sale made, or interest generated. They think to themselves, *"Well that was a waste; I won't go back to that event."* They continue to pop in on various events but soon become frustrated believing networking, well, just doesn't work.

This is so short sighted. After reading Golden Keys 1-4 by now you can probably figure out why. In order for people to like us, to trust us with their business, or to want to refer their friends or family to us, they need to know us. Getting to know someone and building trust takes time. Especially when it comes to those big ticket businesses like buying a home, financial investing, or hiring an expensive coach. Be willing to invest the time into the relationship. Choose a few networking events in your community and commit to attending regularly. Get to know the people there. Meet up for coffee to learn more about what people do.

See if there is someone you know who you could refer to them. I guarantee they will want to return the favor. If you genuinely like them, their service and feel comfortable, offer to share them on your social media. For example take a picture and caption it, *"Having coffee with Susie Smith and learning how she has been helping people with their life insurance needs for 6+ years!"* Wouldn't you love it if someone did that for you? Be the kind of person you want others to be for you. When a new person shows up at your regular networking group go out of your way not just to talk to them, but to introduce them to the rest of the group. Make them feel included. No relationship happens over night.

Most people don't go on a first date and decide to get married. It takes time to get to know someone, and networking is no different. (Although less life changing!) Don't get frustrated after one or two events. When people start to see your face over and over again they will want to get to know you. You will become credible and worthy of referrals. Start with the relationship and build to the business.

I encourage you to take these Golden Keys and put them into practice this week. Knowledge is useful only if acted upon. There is no better time than *now* to start networking. Grab a friend who also wants to expand their network and check out the different events in your area. Find a few and just go. Showing up is half the battle. Be authentic, be genuine, but most importantly be *you*. Let people get to know the real you, the person, not the business. Focus on building relationships and the business will follow. Remember, it's about building *mutually* beneficial relationships. This is a two-way street.

Trust that when you truly network with an others-focused attitude, naturally you, and your business, will benefit too. As the saying goes, *"A simple hello could lead to a million things."* Happy networking!

Tara Geraghty

About the author

Tara is a highly ambitious, resourceful and performance-driven motivational speaker, business owner & acclaimed domestic violence activist. When Tara started in direct sales at 20 years old she found herself immersed in the world of personal development.

She quickly rose to the top of her field, earning numerous accolades and company awards. She soon began teaching, mentoring and coaching women from around the country on how to build successful businesses.

For over 20 years Tara has taught thousands of women through weekly live workshops, training calls, and now webinars. She is the author of, *"From*

Being to Living: A Christian Life Workbook," "Making Cancer Fun," and *"I'm a Miracle Kid."* A domestic violence survivor and mother to a childhood cancer survivor, Tara now speaks at numerous non-profits and seminars, sharing her heart for hope, faith, & gratitude in the midst of life's biggest challenges.

You can reach Tara at: pinkheartinc@mail.com

And follow her at:

www.linkedin.com/in/taragmk

www.facebook.com/tarasvoice

www.instagram.com/taragmk

www.twitter.com/tarasvoice

www.makingcancerfun.com

Marketing Your Business To New Clients

Tabitha Jean Naylor

Imagine your business has a secret formula. This formula comprises of ingredients – or marketing strategies – that make your brand successful, drawing in customers and building a base. While no single marketing method works for every business, there are general rules to follow when developing your formula.

In this chapter, we're going to discuss the creation of this formula through communication with your target audience, understanding and interpreting data, and establishing a unique voice that your customers will remember for years to come.

Even though your formula will differ from that of other businesses, there is one blanket rule to remember – the concept of a starving crowd.

This direct marketing formula has three steps:

- Find a starving crowd.
- Find out what they want.
- Sell them exactly what they want.

To illustrate the concept, we'll pretend your business is a pizzeria. When asked what advantages your shop should have over the competition, you might list location, quality toppings, competitive pricing, and convenient hours. While these features are important, the right secret formula (in other words, the right marketing plan) will come first.

Your pizzeria doesn't need impressive features to get customers through the door, though it helps. More than anything, it needs a starving crowd of pizza-lovers. The right formula will focus on finding those pizza-lovers and bringing them to the forefront.

Put simply, your ultimate marketing goal is to establish communication with those who strongly desire your product or service already, rather than creating desire yourself.

Tools of the Trade

Direct marketers from the late twentieth century would give an arm and a leg for the marketing tools available to entrepreneurs today, many of which we take for granted.

Google, for example, can provide targeted data to tell you what's working, what isn't, how much time customers are spending on your page, how many customers are jumping from your page right away, where your traffic is coming from, and what websites are linking to you.

Your autoresponder (an email marketing tool designed to streamline and personalize the process of sending thousands of emails) can slice your subscriber list and generate an email campaign that reads more like a personal note than a piece of marketing.

Finally, social media organizers can pool several accounts onto an efficient calendar, allowing you to schedule posts and share data with ease.

Many of these applications are free. Today, entrepreneurs find themselves flooded with data that can be harvested to locate and communicate with their starving crowd.

Communicating With Your Crowd

Would you want to receive emails from a company that were clearly meant for a huge audience? Probably not. These messages are rarely tailored to your desires and often feel impersonal. Your target audience may include hundreds of thousands of people, but your message needs to focus on the individual.

At the heart of all marketing campaigns is a singular goal – gain the trust of your prospect. Speaking to each prospect as an individual, rather than a small piece of the pie, will enhance your ability to earn that trust. Once you obtain it, you'll have a loyal customer.

There are several factors that play into the personalization of your marketing strategy, including the medium you choose, your voice, and your method of delivery. In the rest of this chapter, we'll discuss:

- Creating your message.
- Understanding the data available to you.
- Choosing an appropriate medium for communication.

Let's get started!

Creating Your Message

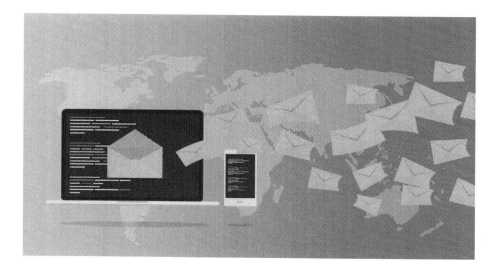

Before you can share your message, you need to create and understand it. This is sometimes the most difficult part of marketing.

In this section, we'll discuss several important topics, including building a proposition, analyzing the competition, avoiding common pitfalls, finding your voice, securing your language, and growing in style.

Building a Proposition

The marketing process begins with a Unique Selling Proposition (USP) that outlines the benefit of purchasing your product. What separates you from the competition?

Sometimes, choosing a USP means selling more than your product. For example, Coca Cola offers refreshment, not soda. Revlon sells hope, not makeup. Walmart sells bargains, not groceries. What benefit are you selling?

Start by deciding what, exactly, your target audience is starving to have. This may take some effort. If you have a list of subscribers or contacts, send a survey. Include questions about why each individual chose your business. You'll want to leave plenty of blank space for comments.

Other methods include:

- Visiting relevant forums and social media groups to see what topics or needs are trending.
- Investing in a targeted survey through applications like SurveyMonkey.
- Speaking with customers face-to-face.

As you review the results, remember that your product or service satisfies the needs of your customer – not you. Whatever your audience says, you'll need to listen carefully and respond accordingly in your next marketing campaign.

Get Familiar With Your Competition

Once you have a general idea of what your audience is looking for in your product, carefully analyze the competition to see how that need is being met. Is the message convincing? Does your competitor focus on benefits rather than features? How would you encourage them to improve? Take these potential improvements and apply them to your own marketing campaign.

You can also obtain feedback from the customers of your competitor by visiting review websites to see what comments are left and how your competitor responds to the review. Note that you should *never* respond negatively to a customer review, no matter how poorly it reflects on your business.

Once you feel familiar with the USP of your competitors, the time has come to develop one of your own.

Focus Your Power, Not Your Price

You've heard the concept before.

"The gas station down the street wants $2.78 a gallon. I'm going to open a gas station and lower my price to $1.25 a gallon. Everyone will come to my station and I'll make a huge profit!"

But running a business isn't as simple as accepting bottom dollar for your product. There are legal and financial responsibilities to recognize. Not to mention that, if your uniqueness is based solely on price, your competition will follow, starting a race to the bottom that usually ends with someone leaving the market altogether.

Instead of going down that road, take an honest look at your business and identify how you can obtain power by standing out.

Your Voice, Your Brand

When many business owners think about branding, they picture a logo or slogan. While these are important parts of your brand, your voice is actually more important.

Voice, in terms of marketing, is the tone and language you use when creating content. If an advertisement has no logo and no slogan, will your customer know it came from you? The right voice makes this goal obtainable.

Why is voice important? There are several reasons.

- It establishes a personality for your brand.
- It expresses the people behind the brand, developing a connection between the reader and the company on a human level.
- Consistent trust is built through a consistent voice. Familiarity makes it easier to believe what you've been told.
- Decisions made about your voice will set you apart from the competition, making your business more memorable to your prospects.

Think carefully about your voice. How will you communicate with your target audience?

Language – It's Everything

There are three components of language that you should remember when developing your marketing content.

First, speak the language of your target audience. For the vast majority of businesses, a conversational voice is appropriate. However, if you fill a specific niche (such as selling sportscars to collectors), you'll want to use industry-specific language. Formal language is often viewed as impersonal, but it can also showcase authority. Use it sparingly.

Second, avoid technical jargon whenever possible. Jargon is speech that means nothing to the average reader. Some marketing jargon, for example, includes CPI, CPM, SEO, ROI, gated content, inbound marketing, and lead generation. You might not understand what these phrases mean, but the marketing community does.

Jargon includes words or phrases used between yourself and employees during business hours. If you choose to use acronyms, define them and explain them. The same is true for important terminology that cannot be removed from your content without dismantling the message.

Finally, make sure your content speaks to the individual, not the masses. Anonymity eliminates all sense of responsibility, ensuring your prospects won't feel obligated to follow through by scheduling an appointment or making a purchase.

Growing With Grace

As your business grows, you'll begin adding staff members and contractors to your collection. During this process, the voice you've carefully developed may fall by the wayside. The more people involved in your content creation, the more likely your voice will be diluted or changed.

To avoid this problem, create a style guide. This guide will be handed to each person added to the content creation team, guaranteeing that all parties understand the values of your company and how you conduct your business. Include copies of successful content from the past and answer questions thoroughly. This way, your voice will grow as your company expands.

Understanding Available Data

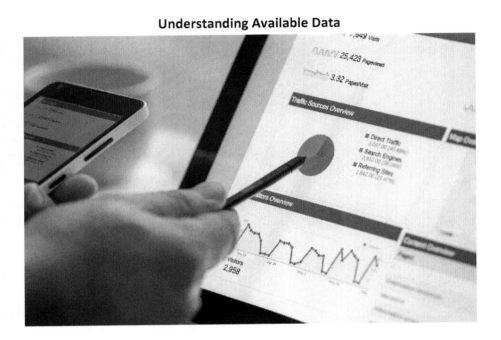

In the late twentieth century, mailing lists were the medium of choice. The quality of the list ultimately determined how many sales would be made. Outdated lists meant instant junk mail and a waste of valuable resources. The most successful mailing lists included audience members who specifically requested information – and therefore waited for the mail to arrive.

Today, everything is done digitally. Entrepreneurs are able to collect millions of bits of data through a variety of platforms and applications. Large computer companies hire scientists, mathematicians, and technicians who specialize in gathering data, designing an algorithm to understand the data, and presenting their findings in an organized fashion.

You can accomplish all three of these steps at once by finding the right website for your data needs. There are many options available to you, some of which we'll discuss in the following sections.

Using an Autoresponder

By far, your most valuable marketing asset is your email list – today's version of the mailing list. Using harvested data and deductive reasoning, you can significantly increase your conversion rate through enhanced communication.

The process of building and organizing your list is critical. While you can create an email marketing plan manually, we highly suggest using an autoresponder. These applications have dozens of useful features and relatively few (if any) drawbacks.

Start by subscribing to the autoresponder service of your choice. Autoresponders can segment your prospects, automatically send appropriate email messages, and much more.

For example, if a member of your target audience supplies his or her email to receive your newsletter, that email will be added to a general prospect list *and* a newsletter list. Whenever you publish a newsletter, the system will automatically send a copy to everyone on the newsletter list. The same is true for any general promotion.

Autoresponders have the ability to track the activity of each email address user. For example, you can determine the level of interest a single customer has in your offer. You'll know if the email was opened, if a link was clicked, and if an action took place. This can help you understand what your customer wants, allowing you to build more groups for specific offers.

The more specific your marketing plan, the more valuable the results. Your autoresponder will provide data on the effectiveness of your messages. You'll quickly learn what concepts are working and what concepts need work.

Using Google Analytics

To start learning about the advantages of Google, install Google Analytics on your website. Once the installation is complete, you'll have access to a flood of useful data.

Why is Google so wonderful?

- The analytics program is completely free, supplying useful data for everyone.
- You can learn how visitors find your website.
- You can read an evaluation of specific pages, helping you improve your website.
- You will have access to demographic information on your visitors.
- You will know what websites are linking to yours.
- The program will list keywords often used to reach your website.

If you just created your website, you'll need to wait for actionable data. Without traffic, data cannot be collected.

Using Your Customer Base

Looking to expand your established business? Use your customer base for assistance.

While most business owners desire new customers and focus the majority of their marketing budget toward getting them, lead generation is nowhere near as profitable as repeat business.

Obtaining new customers isn't cheap. Online advertising, cold calls, email campaigns, and other marketing expenses add up quickly, making some owners wonder, "Is this even worth it?"

According to a 2010 Marketing Metrics Report, the odds of closing a new customer range from five percent to twenty percent. The rate for repeat business, on the other hand, ranges from sixty percent to seventy percent.

Existing customers already know and trust you. They've spent a significant amount of money on you. Rather than going through the acquisition process again, simply give them an opportunity (or a reason) to come back.

Using a CRM System

Do you have a Customer Relationship Management (CRM) System? If not, you need one – fast. A CRM System will manage your sales process, strengthen your relationships, and serve as a central reporting center for all of the data that comes your way from marketing, customer service, sales, and social media.

When using a CRM System, you'll have access to the complete history of your customers. What did they buy? How much did they buy? When did they buy? What issues were faced? What referrals were given? This data will give you a complete profile of your starving crowd – and what they're anxious to have next.

This way, using your current customers, you can obtain new ones.

Using Loyalty Programs and Customer Advocates

Your customer base has a significant impact on your bottom line. Give your customers an opportunity to become advocates.

A satisfied customer will, without being asked, share your information with those in his or her circle of influence. This is more effective than your most expensive marketing campaign – and it's free!

The best way to encourage this behavior is to offer an impressive, unbeatable experience or product. There are, however, other ways to spread customer engagement, including social media pages, online reviews, and loyalty programs.

Social media is a highly effective conduit for customer engagement. You can build a community on Facebook, LinkedIn, Twitter, and other popular websites. The key to success is being engaged yourself. You'll need to choose someone to be the voice of the company; someone willing to actively participate. Otherwise, your pages will simply be viewed as advertising. You can also encourage your customers to sing your praises online by asking them to review you through Google, Yelp, LinkedIn, or Angie's List. Comments can be requested through receipts, invoices, shipping fliers, and social media posts. Never ignore an opportunity to ask for feedback.

The final draw of customer engagement, loyalty programs, has unlimited potential. Many large businesses have free-to-join programs that save money for repeat customers, inspiring them to return over and over again.

To put it simply, take advantage of the business you already have. You don't need to pay for it – and you'll get more profit from it.

The Importance of Medium Choice

In 1964, Marshall McLuhan published a book detailing the importance of "medium" in society. At the time, popular mediums included theatre, records, movies, radio, television, and print.

Today, there are *many* mediums to choose from, making it more difficult than ever to choose the right one. Your message must be delivered consistently to build your brand and establish trust with your customers. What medium will help you accomplish that goal? After all, not all communication channels are made equally.

In addition to the added computer medium, the internet introduces dozens of platforms for your brand and your voice. Before diving into social media, carefully research each platform to find the best fit. For example, local businesses tend to benefit from Facebook (which offers a small, community feel) while large brand names tend to benefit similarly from Instagram.

Start by studying your existing customers. Where does your target audience spend time? That platform is where you'll get your edge.

In this section, we'll discuss a variety of medium options, including email marketing, podcasts, blogs, and social media.

Email Marketing

While companies like Google would love to claim that email marketing is dead, the practice is alive, well, and thriving. There are few things you cannot do with a strongly constructed email series.

Email marketing offers the highest ROI (Return on Investment) of any communication channel. Estimations show that businesses, on average, see more than four thousand dollars of revenue for every hundred dollars invested in email marketing campaigns.

Why does email marketing work?

- Like social media, your email inbox can be addictive. The average user will check his or her email several times a day, while more active users will check several dozen.

- When we spend time online, our attention span is extremely limited. Emails provide quiet, private communication, allowing you to communicate directly with your target audience.
- Unlike social media campaigns, which are limited by the rules of the platform, your email marketing campaign can follow whatever rules you choose. Facebook isn't using an algorithm to determine who views your emails – and Google can't control your ability to be seen.
- Email drives a significant amount of traffic. An email can lead to your most recent blog post, newsletter, or social media page.
- When companies use an autoresponder, they can track every detail of an individual email address. You'll quickly learn how to target your key demographic.

SEO/SEM

SEO stands for Search Engine Optimization. SEM stands for Search Engine Marketing. These are, ultimately, two sides of the same coin. The only difference? SEO is free. SEM is not.

When you search on Google, you'll usually see three or four listings separated from the bunch. They'll appear at the top of the page, to the right of your search results, or to the left. These listings are paid advertisements.

Each time a link is clicked, the advertiser is charged by Google. These spots are purchased through bids placed by businesses on specific keywords. The business with the highest bid – and the most relevant content – wins.

SEM can drive a great deal of traffic to your website in a short amount of time. On the flip side, it can quickly sap your marketing budget. You should also note that consumers are getting wise. A fair percentage of the time, users will ignore paid advertisements altogether in search of more organic content.

SEO offers a top-spot in that organic content, and it involves an awful lot of legwork. The goal is to have your page rank high (first or second listing) for specific keywords. Content published on your website can help improve your ranking, but there are other factors considered in the algorithm used by Google and Bing.

SEO is a moving target. Only a handful of employees at Google understand the algorithm being used, and that algorithm can change *at any time*, rendering the work you've done meaningless.

Common advice given to business owners is this: Make a genuinely useful website, and your ranking will handle itself. Convince your visitors that your content supplies real, coveted value.

If you decide to invest in SEO, hire an expert in the field. It can be difficult, and sometimes impossible, to succeed without professional assistance.

In an ideal world, SEO and SEM complement one another. SEM can boast SEO, making it sustainable long-term. Still, your time and money are likely better spent in less bloated areas of marketing.

Subscriptions

When you offer quality content, you can reap the rewards associated with subscriptions. When followers receive emails from your blog, podcast, or channel, you'll get real-time results showcasing your popularity.

Remember that, in order to run a successful subscription campaign, you need to keep content coming. Once you have a fair number of followers, they'll expect content on a weekly basis. Don't ruin that commitment – or you'll quickly lose their interest and their trust.

Social Media

Social media is a great and powerful marketing tool. It can also be your downfall. There are so many websites serving so many purposes that becoming overwhelmed is almost a given.

Freshly started businesses should begin establishing themselves on Facebook and LinkedIn. Once you've mastered these platforms, consider exploring other avenues of communication with your target audience.

The purpose of social media is to establish a community between like-minded people. You can't preach to your audience – you need to have a conversation with them. That means responding to comments and reviews, making consistent updates, and ensuring you have the staff to handle a complex campaign.

There are more than a hundred social media websites. New contenders arrive on a weekly basis. While none of these platforms can be ignored as a potential marketing resource, you can't possibly establish a following on all of them. You need to select a community that offers engagement with your starving crowd.

Facebook, LinkedIn, Instagram, and YouTube are used frequently by business owners across the country and around the world.

- Facebook has more than two billion users, many of them highly engaged with their online community.
- LinkedIn is the premiere networking website, allowing you to push your brand in front of hundreds of commercial customers.
- Instagram has a strong following and offers a photo-centric platform for visual driven businesses.
- YouTube communities use channels to deliver messages and establish a voice.

Whichever platform you choose, remember that social media websites are dripping with distractions. Create a highly targeted campaign that will bring your customers forward.

In Closing

In this chapter, we covered a significant amount of material. There are a few key takeaways to remember:

- Your current customers are an untapped pool of free marketing. Take advantage of them through loyalty programs, social media pages, and review requests.
- The voice of your brand matters *just as much* as your slogan and your logo, if not more.
- Data gathered by Google Analytics and other affordable applications can change the way you market forever.
- Investing in a CRM (Customer Relationship Management) System can streamline everything you do, including sales, marketing, and social media.
- Choosing the right medium for your message is essential.
- SEO (Search Engine Optimization) is best attempted with a professional.
- Invest your social media time on Facebook, LinkedIn, Instagram, and YouTube.
- Measure everything you do.
- Improve based on those measurements to make your marketing campaign better and better every time.

Tabitha Jean Naylor

About the author

Tabitha Jean Naylor is the owner of TabithaNaylor.com and a certified Inbound Marketing Consultant with over a decade of experience in both B2B and B2C markets.

A self-described digital marketing machine, she prides herself in her ability to craft text that generates action. Her intimate knowledge of how sales and marketing go hand-in-hand has resulted in a variety of successful campaigns for start-ups through NASDAQ traded companies.

Ms. Naylor holds a dual bachelor degree in Political Science and International Business from West Virginia University, where she graduated magna cum laude. Her experience brings a unique perspective to connecting with the online world community, especially given the variety of projects she has spearheaded. Her areas of expertise include Branding, Content Marketing, Copywriting, Graphic Design and SMM.

The New Entrepreneurial Mindset

Eddie Blass

There was a time that the archetype role model of 'The Entrepreneur' was the likes of Donald Trump and Alan Sugar; the so called self-made business men who had made it so good they got their own TV shows setting entrepreneurial challenges to a group of potential 'apprentices[1]'. They represent the ultimate success according to the dominant white male paradigm in a capitalist society. They've played every dodge and system they can to ensure they remain millionaires, regardless of who they leave in their wake, or how they go about business. Ultimately, if you didn't agree with them – 'you're fired!'

I mentioned in this introduction the 'dominant white male paradigm' in capitalist society and I just want to revisit that statement now. This model of success that Donald Trump represents is the model we are conditioned to accept as we grow up in Western societies (those subscribing to a capitalist, market driven economic model). Success is related to money; ergo the more you are personally worth, the more successful you are. The expectation is that it will be men who are the representations of this success, and while there are some women in the mix, they are the exception not the rule, and there is a plethora of data to support this. While diversity and the glass ceiling are more commonly challenged within

---

[1] Donald Trump hosted a TV reality show called 'The Apprentice' in the US, which was then replicated with Alan Sugar in the UK. At the end of each week, the poorest performer, in the eyes of the host, was 'fired'.

the corporate world, the world of start-ups and entrepreneurs is way behind[2].

This view of success stemming from a monetary base is also perpetuated by the majority of educational offerings that developed for entrepreneurs. Most University courses for entrepreneurs are the equivalent of an MBA for small businesses or start-ups, and do nothing to challenge this dominant model. Their curriculum includes all the traditional business subjects, in their requisite silos, but in this instance applied to the entrepreneurial or small business context. That is not to say that every budding entrepreneur should not know something about business, but the context in which it is explored should perhaps be challenged. What if it were taught in the context of 'this is how many people do business today – how are you going to disrupt that?' rather than 'how are you going to succeed within that?'

So, not surprisingly, the revolution and new entrepreneurial mindset is developing its groundswell from the bottom up, stemming from the models of the collaborative economy[3], self-organising networks, and with the support of governments starting to panic that the future of work is uncertain for future generations. Where are the jobs going to come from if people don't create them for themselves?

---

[2] See for example: https://www.inc.com/stephanie-chung/breaking-the-glass-ceiling-as-a-female-entrepreneur.html; https://www.theguardian.com/small-business-network/2017/jan/11/women-led-startups-smashing-glass-ceiling-investment; http://theconversation.com/are-women-less-likely-to-become-entrepreneurs-65863.

[3] See for example: https://www.entrepreneur.com/article/254725; http://sloanreview.mit.edu/article/crowd-based-capitalism-empowering-entrepreneurs-in-the-sharing-economy/; http://www.huffingtonpost.com/marty-zwilling/be-a-winning-entrepreneur_b_7233874.html .

There are number of tipping points that we are reaching in society that are driving this shifting mindset. The first shift is that post- global financial crisis Western societies are unlikely to see the next generation improving on the wealth of their parents[4]. As people are living longer and the burden on pension funds and health provisions increases, the reality for the generation moving into the workplace now, and future generations thereafter, is that the demographics are unsustainable with the concept of on-going economic growth[5].

Home ownership amongst many young people, for example, is becoming an aspiration rather than an expectation, and many young people are remaining living with their parents, or in shared rental accommodation[6]. Such communal arrangements, while stemming from a potential 'negative' in our dominant white male paradigm, will shift societal thinking and experiences away from the purely competitive 'look out for number one', to one of understanding and looking out for 'the other' in addition to the self. For example, if you're doing well but cannot share that success with the people you are living with or friends with, there is no real celebration of success. Likewise, if your success is at the expense of your friends or the people you live with, it is very bitter success indeed.

So through this tipping point in housing affordability, we are seeing a redefinition of how success is celebrated in society, away from being the sole winner in competition with everyone else, to someone who is looking to share this success with others. This is a subtle shift, but from sharing

---

[4] See for example: https://www.rba.gov.au/publications/bulletin/2009/may/pdf/bu-0509-4.pdf; https://tasa.org.au/wp-content/uploads/2011/01/Chesters-Jenny.pdf.
[5] See, for example: https://www.environment.gov.au/system/files/resources/5e314999-030b-4754-bcc3-6d1d02661381/files/demographic-panel-report.pdf.
[6] http://thenewdaily.com.au/money/property/2017/04/11/2016-census-home-ownership/.

successful outcomes, we will see the sharing of contributions to successful outcomes.   As people become involved in sharing success, they will naturally want to become involved in creating success.

This might sound obvious, as nobody gets out of bed in the morning wanting to create failure – but until now we have witnessed a society where life has been one big competition, where there are winners and losers.   Now we are moving to a society where winners are more integrated with those 'yet to win', and everyone winning has more appeal than previously.

But this isn't just happening because of the global financial crisis (GFC) and housing affordability; it is also occurring as a result of social media, and the constant sharing and judgements (likes) being granted to us for sharing our successes (and sometimes failures) publicly with our ever growing groups of 'friends'.   While our success could only previously be seen by those in our locality, our family and friends that we physically kept in touch with, we can now celebrate success with thousands of 'followers' on Instagram, 'friends' on Facebook, and the world through Twitter!   More difficult for the more modest amongst us, but a way of keeping people up to date, looped in and contributing to your success through promoting what you are doing to others through 'recommendations', and being a part of your celebrations through 'sharing'.

So, we have the GFC and social media as two contributors to the new entrepreneurial mindset, but it doesn't end there.   The millennials in particular are asking 'why'?[7]   They look at the model of their parents' generation working all the hours they can for money to pay for a lifestyle they are struggling to sustain, and all for what?   Back to the old question of

---

[7] See, for example: http://luckyattitude.co.uk/millennial-characteristics/; http://www.pewresearch.org/topics/millennials/.

what is the meaning of life. And I don't mean this flippantly. More and more people are asking what is the point? Why are they playing this game? And they want to make a difference. The growth of social enterprises, for example, is evidence of this as the for-profit for-good sector, allowing people to gain personal success and societal success consecutively. Social enterprises are a particularly unique challenge to the dominant white male paradigm as they are established within the capitalist framework and boundaries of ownership and for-profit, but then reinvest the profit back into society rather than distributing it to the shareholders. The society becomes the proxy owner or shareholder.

A dissatisfaction with the status quo is arguably the spark at the heart of the new entrepreneurial mindset. The drive is not simply to be rich; and pursuing a business idea simply because it has good market potential does not cut it. While this might have been the model behind the traditional entrepreneurial model, it doesn't answer the 'why' question for the emerging entrepreneur.

Building on the need to answer 'why', there is a surge in women who are returning from maternity leave to the workplace and seeking more than their previous employers can now offer them. Affectionately named the 'mumpreneurs' as a group (although arguably this title is derogatory and sustains the image that mothers returning to work are somehow 'different' to other women in the workplace) this group is growing and finding its voice and inspiration through champions, networks and a new form of short course education offered by previous successes in this field.

A whole industry is forming around start-ups, and entrepreneurs of one form or another contributing to the growth of the start-up movement through offering courses, mentoring, coaching, and in some cases, funding. Given that the data tells us the success rate of entrepreneurs is low (ie around 95% fail), there is a logic here that suggests this industry is founded on failures helping other people fail, but that aside, it is a booming area which again is contributing to the collaborative nature of success, both through development of and celebration of outcomes.

Of particular note in this industry is the growth of incubators and accelerator programs. Incubators offer space and support to start-ups in their very early ideation stage; accelerators are a means of Venture Capital funds accelerating the growth of those ideas they think could actually be strong viable businesses to speed up (or accelerate) their growth in capital value. They are an industry that essentially promotes and tests business ideas to breaking point very quickly, and if they don't break, they claim a potential asset value on the idea which could be way in excess of a 'real' market value, such that the business can then raise more funds on the basis of having succeeded in this element of marketisation. In essence it is the quick route through the maze, bringing you to the end game quickly. Their success rate is higher than the average for a start-up, but keep in mind they are well practiced at the process and vet out those they think won't make it in their recruitment process. Indeed, failing to be accepted into an accelerator could be a first sign of potential danger in your business succeeding in its current model. Make sure you get feedback so you understand why, and then pivot accordingly to succeed.

Phil Nosworthy, of 'The Be Smart Club', posted a short video challenging the notion of the self-made man[8]. He argues that it simply doesn't exist, because behind every so-called self-made man, there are a plethora of people who have made it possible for them to succeed in the way that they have. This includes the farmers that grow the food that person eats, the people who run the company that keeps their phone service going, and so forth. The point he makes is that we are all dependent on each other in some way or another, and hence to single yourself out as self-made

---

[8] https://www.youtube.com/watch?v=1hAZ1h2IgcU

success is a nonsense. In essence, you have succeeded in doing what you are doing because other people's success at what they are doing enables you to do so. Success therefore should be shared as you could not possibly do it alone.

And this is at the heart of the new entrepreneurial mindset. This realisation that it isn't just about you – it is about who you are seeking to serve; who you will succeed with; who you will depend upon; and who you will share with. It is not all about ownership and maximising shareholder value – it is about service and maximising societal outcomes one way or another.

The collaborative mentality amongst the start-up community and networks sees them trading like for like. Lisa Messenger[9] promotes this in her books *'Daring and Disruptive'* and *'Money and Mindfulness'*. While these are far from the academic textbooks you would see on the booklist of your entrepreneurs' courses in business schools, they are full of practical tips for getting yourself going, including trading in a barter market of other start-ups and entrepreneurs. How can you offer each other time and service to the mutual benefit of you both, rather than you both failing because you haven't got the liquidity to buy the services you need? Hers are just one of a selection of offerings of this genre.

Equally when negotiating large scale investment programs, people are starting to consider licensing and equity arrangements rather than upfront payment, so that suppliers have a vested interest in a start-up succeeding. Having some 'skin in the game' so to speak ensures the suppliers commit to the business succeeding, rather than simply committing to providing some goods or services, appropriate or not.

---

[9] Lisa Messenger is the Founder of The Collective Hub, a magazine, network and short course provider for entrepreneurs, offering a message that shifts the dominant pattern of thinking.

So the new entrepreneurial mindset is one of collaborating and sharing for everyone's success; it's one of trading, seeing opportunities, and helping each other, rather than succeeding at the expense of each other; it is customer, service or society driven rather than profit driven, and in looking after the customer or society, they will look after themselves. Unlike the famous declaration by Gordon Gekko in the infamous Oliver Stone film 'Wall Street[10]', 'greed' is not a good word in the new entrepreneurs' vocabulary. So, will this new mindset shift our market based capitalist economies to a new economic paradigm? We are already on the way.

Eddie Blass

Founder and CEO, The Inventorium Pty Ltd

---

[10] This film was about an wall street trader who infamously says the line 'Greed is Good' when discussing illegal insider trading.

About the author

Eddie Blass was a successful career academic, Professor in early Business and Education, who then had cross-university roles to innovate education, and quickly realised that she couldn't bring about the transformation necessary within the system itself. In essence we have taken a 19th century idea designed for the elite, massified it for everyone in the 20th century, and are now delivering it in the 21st century with very little change. So she started thinking, what would people choose to learn and do if we didn't tell them what they had to learn and do?

This is now the heart of Eddie's entrepreneurial endeavours, and she now writes curriculum and works in entrepreneurial education, having had projects with The Collective Hub, Slingshot, Torrens University Australia and was a SA finalist herself in Australia Posts Regional PItchfest with her social enterprise The Inventorium. While able to write to the 'old economic model', her particular specialty is working to develop entrepreneurs for the new emerging economic models such as the collaborative economy.

How to Hack Your Own Franchise Company Start-Up
Rune Sovndahl

The opportunities and challenges of the franchise business model

The franchise business model is one which offers one of the greatest potentials for expansion. More ethical and resulting in a more beneficial working relationship than any company trying to get in on the gig economy model, a franchise business can grow quickly and be self-funding from the very start. But it also presents some serious challenges to those thinking about starting up their own business and run it in this way...

What you'll get out of this chapter

A greater understanding of some of the many potential opportunities and challenges of running your own franchise business. Afterwards, you should also be able to avoid one of the biggest mistakes that people make when starting up their own franchise company:

They expect to quickly rise to a level of a Subway or a McDonalds without putting any work in. Taking a look at a couple of the challenges below should help you understand that no business simply pops into the world in its perfect form. It's taken the owners of McDonalds, Hilton Hotels and other big franchises many, many iterations and tests and improvements to get to where they are now.

Like them, and any business, when you're starting your own franchise company you will have many failures. Hopefully not critical, company-destroying failures, but many small, everyday failures and setbacks. Only by expecting these and planning for them, and by having an attitude that accepts failure and strives to overcome and learn from it will you eventually succeed.

A wise man once said, "fall seven times and get up eight".

It's an attitude of resilience that as a new entrepreneur you'll almost certainly become intimately familiar with. Perhaps this chapter might even help you to avoid a few of them.

Why listen to the advice you see here?

This chapter represents the fruit of the many failures and successes I've had growing my own franchise company - Fantastic Services - from nothing eight years ago to a £32 million turnover business today. From a chance meeting at a party between two strangers - my business partner Anton (who had the skills and experience of the industry) and myself (with skills and experience in marketing and technology) the company has expanded far beyond what we originally envisioned when we were just two guys with a shared laptop and mobile phone on a coffee shop sofa.

In large part, the topics here fall under the category of *"things I wish I'd known when starting out"*. I hope they'll point you towards making smart decisions when you start up your own franchise.

The Challenges and Opportunities of Starting Your Own Franchise Business

Opportunity: Everyone gets to do the thing that they're the expert in

Let's start with what I see as one of the main benefits of a properly working franchise system:

No time is wasted by someone who's trying to do a job which they're not an expert in.

If you've ever tried to do a job which you haven't been trained in or had experience in yourself you'll know that it can be done. But it takes time, it often takes practice to get the "knack" of whatever you're doing, and odds on you aren't going to produce an end result which is half as good as anyone with even a modicum of training.

By determining where the expertise lies in your franchise you make sure that the right jobs get done by the right people. No working hours are wasted. Work is done to the highest standards. Greater profit ensues.

This means that your franchisees should be free to deliver their services (the things that they're the expert in) while you provide all the support they need to do it (the things you're the expert in). In almost every case this will come down to:

1. **The training** they need in order to deliver those services effectively
2. **The marketing** they need in order to have customers to deliver those services to

As a franchisor you'll also need to provide other things of course:

- An established name and reputation
- A business concept and Unique Selling Points which speak to your market
- All of the processes which make your franchise the most effective one on the market
- Brand names and trademarks

But in general, you should be providing almost any general assistance your franchisee needs to grow their business. Because if your franchisee could provide the expertise to effectively market and support their business at the same time as run it, they wouldn't need you. You're there to give them everything they need in order to run their business effectively and efficiently.

We've found this to mean we also provide things like:

- Vehicle purchase loans
- Equipment purchase loans
- An in-house app which tracks their jobs
- Centralised customer service and handling all communication with customers
- Medical consultations

In return, each of your franchisees will need to provide:

- The go-getting attitude required to succeed
- A commitment to honesty and reliability
- Some experience in the field (*although this isn't really a requirement. After all, you're going to be providing them with extensive training...*)

Opportunity: Marketing your franchise

This is something that it's absolutely critical that you get right. Some franchise companies allow their individual franchisees to run their own marketing operations, but this is a mistake in my experience. The skills and hard work of your franchisee in delivering their services are only going to be diluted if they also need to spend the time and energy researching their market and selling their services too.

Your franchise marketing should be handled by you at the franchisor level. Speaking from knowledge of the way Fantastic Services has grown, the ability to find our franchisees consistent business on a daily basis - achieved through effective marketing of the brand - has been one of the biggest draws bringing us the talented franchisees we need in order to grow. I think I'm right in saying that we were the first hybrid that chose to do our own marketing and I really can't recommend it enough as a strategy to take on board.

We use all potential channels that have proven effective for the industry we're in:

- Social media channels
- Media and PR
- Partnering with local bloggers
- Local search and SEO
- Creating and sending out weekly email and SMS campaigns to domestic and corporate clients
- Pay per click advertising
- Trade shows

Our Media and Outreach team goes above and beyond the usual activities you might expect from a marketing department. They've let us:

- Feature in magazines and newspapers (online and print) and blogs - The Metro, The Telegraph. The Sunday Times, The Daily Mail, The Evening Standard, The Sun, Forbes, City A.M., Elite Franchise Magazine, BQ Live, Square Mile, and more.
- Appear on radio and podcast show programmes - TRE Radio, Share Radio, and several others.
- Appear on TV - Sky News, CNN, BBC, Reuters, and others.

We've used all of these mentions to raise brand awareness and to talk more about the specific franchise model we use. This has led to a consistent uptake in the number of people using our services, and the number of people who express an interest and go on to be franchise holders of ours in their own right.

This is all designed to show you that you need to perform extensive, well-targeted marketing using all the channels which you've determined are effective at selling your goods and services. This is a huge part of what you need to provide your franchisees as a franchisor, and to grow your business in general.

For your industry the exact marketing channels you use might be different, so you'll need to research which channels convert effectively in order to efficiently target your marketing spend.

Challenge: Enforcing compliance with your franchise agreement terms

Your franchise agreement is the most important document and legal foundation for the structure of your company. It will lay out the responsibilities and duties of you to your franchisees and vice versa. But it's one thing to write a smart document, and it's another to enforce it.

Critically, it's another thing to enforce it without being a tyrant - without stifling one of the potentially fantastic outcomes of having many business leaders operating under the same franchise: The fact that anyone - any franchisee or any technician working for any franchisee - in the entire company could come up with an innovation which improves the effectiveness or profitability of the franchise as a whole.

Encouraging your professionals to contribute to the success of the company and rewarding them when they have an idea which might lead to further innovation is a great way to maximise their engagement with their role and to improve their happiness (an incredibly important point which we'll talk about below as a final point).

That said, you do need to make sure that your franchisees don't treat the smart and efficient market-beating processes and systems that you've instituted as suggestions that they can take or leave. Some of the most difficult franchisees to deal with are those who still want to get things done "their way" despite joining your network.

One of the ways in which we avoid this situation is to choose our franchisees very carefully (again this links into the final point, so see more about it later). But we've also discovered that group learning is a highly effective tool for getting through to even these difficult individuals. This means we provide extensive learning sessions with franchisees from many different parts of the network in the same groups, seminars and so on. Many of these are conducted by trainers we've brought in who are used to working with Fortune 100 companies because it's always worth ensuring the training you provide is of the highest quality you can.

By effectively training your franchisees they should come to accept that they need to:

- Comply with the terms and conditions outlined by the brand (including trademark, branding, corporate policy, dress code, and so on)

- Follow the quality standards set by the brand

- Trust someone else with the marketing, sales and IT

- Discuss and agree upon jointly decided growth and development plans, not go their own way

Training can also assist you with another one of the major challenges of running a franchise business...

Opportunity and Challenge: Ensuring quality across your franchise network
Linked to solving the challenge of enforcing compliance with your franchise agreement is that of ensuring that all of your franchisees understand that they need to deliver services of a certain quality.

The link, of course, is proper training.

One of the main advantages of a franchise is that you all rise together. Conversely, of course, it's all too easy to fall together too. One poorly performing franchise operation can quickly tarnish the reputation of the company as a whole. At the risk of belabouring the point, let's use the example of a fast food business:

You walk into a fast food outlet and buy a burger. You're met with rude staff, dirty counters and poorly cooked food. You won't be visiting any of the company's outlets in other cities - even if they're run by different franchisors who have helpful staff, are scrupulous about cleanliness and know how to cook a mean burger. The brand is now ruined in your eyes.

This is where the challenge of ensuring quality across your entire franchise network becomes apparent. As your company grows it's only going to become more important. You can't visit every single one of your franchise locations every day or be watching over each franchisee's shoulder every minute. You need to have provided them with the tools they need to deliver the quality of service you expect by themselves.

That means quality control of course, but it also means training. Constant, centralised and properly assessed training.

It's a lesson we learned early when starting Fantastic Services - in fact, it's one of the reasons we started the company in the first place. We deliver the training from a centralised location, which we call the Fantastic Academy. The courses we provide are in line with what our franchisees and the individual technicians working for them will need to know in order to grow their businesses and deliver a reliably high standard of service quality.

The exact training courses that you deliver will obviously depend on your own industry, but simply trusting that your new franchisee will deliver services of the standard you expect simply because they say they will is a risk that you cannot afford to take.

Failing to ensure quality across the network is the reason that many franchise businesses fail.

The Main Challenge and Opportunity - 360 Degree Happiness and Hiring the Right People

Building a successful and effective relationship between yourself and your franchisees is perhaps the most important part of building a franchise system which really works. In many ways, the other challenges and opportunities - letting the right people do the right job, effective marketing, enforcing compliance with your franchise's processes, guaranteeing quality, and all the myriad others - depend on the strength of this relationship.

There's one big secret to making it work:

Happiness.

Bear with me here; there's an unassailable logic to this that goes far deeper than the slightly wishy-washy statement this appears to be on the surface.

To get on board with this notion you need to understand some things about being an entrepreneur. You'll probably know this already, but they bear repeating:

1) Being a successful entrepreneur takes hard work

First up, if you're expecting starting your own franchise company to allow you to ride to success on the back of the work of other people, let me tell you, you are going to be in for a big surprise when you get going!

Running a franchise business is an exhausting job. For me personally, it's taken a lot of sacrifices to get to where we are today, and you'll no doubt experience the same thing as you grow your own company. Late nights and hard days aren't the least of it.

2) You can't do it alone

You need to hire the right people. You need a team which is going to want to work almost as hard as you do. Plus, it's worth bearing in mind that you're going to be working with these people, including your franchisees, day in and day out for - hopefully - many years to come. If they're not happy, they're going to make you unhappy. And that may well be the straw that breaks the camel's back in terms of what you can stand to give to make your business work.

I know for a fact that if we hadn't managed to build a team at Fantastic Services that were as dedicated to making it succeed as I was, I probably would have called it a day many years ago.

But over and above that aspect, as an experienced leader, you'll know that happy and engaged people work better and give more to their work than those who are just going through the motions, not caring about what they do.

3) It's a two-way street

Just in case this hasn't been emphasised enough by this point, any good franchisor-franchisee relationship will mean the provision of support as well as the expectation of hard work.

By making sure your franchisees are happy, you're helping them give you the very best that they can. This will be helped by the fact they're:

- **The experts they need to be** - in order to provide high-quality services
- **Supported by you in all other respects** - marketing and constant innovation of the most effective processes are amongst the most important of these.

The parts of the job that you're each the expert in should complement each other in order to create a winning mix.

At Fantastic Services all of this combines into what we call our 360 Degree Happiness Philosophy. It means that everyone - the founders, CEO, marketers, sales team, franchisees, suppliers, individual professionals on the front lines - get what they need out of their job. I heartily encourage you to create something similar for your own company.

It'll provide a great deal of the support you need as you take advantage of the opportunities and try to avoid the challenges of starting up your own franchise business.

Rune Sovndahl

About the author

Rune Sovndahl is co-founder and CEO of Fantastic Services - an online platform where clients can book professional domestic services providers such as plumbers, gardeners and cleaners. Mr Sovndahl, who is Danish, moved to London almost 20 years ago to go to Southbank University. Following completion of his degree he was accepted onto a graduate programme with British Telecom and most recently he worked for lastminute.com as Group SEO Manager.

He has built his domestic services business from scratch to a point where they serve 230,000 clients in London, the South East and the North West of England. With £32m turnover, it is easily the largest home services provider in London, yet the company has been self-financed since the outset. As well as the UK, Fantastic Services is already established as a leader in Australia and the USA.

Social Media Marketing For Businesses

Katina Beveridge

Digital marketing, especially social media, has greatly changed the business landscape around the world. From advertising techniques to reaching out to customers to aftersales, businesses found themselves thrust into a world where everything is real time.

When customers have a question, they want immediate answers. If there are concerns, they want instant resolution. When they need to buy something, they want to find out where and how they can purchase and for how much. Businesses have to cope with these needs to be able to survive.

So businesses have turned to social media to address these concerns of the consumers.

What is social media?

According to Searchengineland, "Social media itself is a catch-all term for sites that may provide radically different social actions." Others refer to social media as a means of interaction or a channel through which people create, share, and/or exchange information and ideas in virtual communities and networks.

Popular social media platforms include:

- Facebook (1.9 billion users)
- WhatsApp (1.2 billion users as of February 2017)
- Messenger (1.2 billion users as of April 2017)

- YouTube (1 billion users)
- WeChat/Weixin (889 million users)
- QQ (869 million users)
- Instagram (700 million users)
- Qzone (638 million users)
- Twitter (328 million users)
- Tumblr (550 million users)
- Weibo (313 million users)
- Snapchat (300 million users)
- Pinterest (150 million users)
- LinkedIn (106 million users)

Benefits of Social Media for Businesses

We all know that social media has a lot of advantages when it comes to running and growing a business. We've listed down the benefits of using social media for your business.

1. Get to know your customers more. One of the most important aspect of running a business is getting to know who your targeted market is. Social media provides business owners with valuable customer insights that they can use in creating a marketing plan or campaign. Social media platforms generate a huge amount of real time data about your customers. Everyday there are billions of content posted on social media channels like Facebook, Twitter and Instagram which provide business owners a wealth of information about their customers. These posts – videos, pictures, comments, likes – allow you to know more about your audience – who they are, what they like, what they don't like and what they think about your company or brand. As a business owner, you can gather and use these data to make strategic business decisions.
2. Increase brand awareness. Having genuine social media presence makes it easier for your potential customers to find you and reach

out to you. Engaging with your customers on social media increases customer retention and improves brand loyalty. Whether you're answering questions from customers or sending out promo information, reaching out to your customers through social media opens up a communication channel between you and you customers.

3. Targeted ads, real time results. One of the disadvantages of traditional advertising is that it is difficult to evaluate whether your ad is effective or not. In the case of social media advertising, you can run targeted ads and get results real time. You have an idea whether your ad is delivering and if not, you have the option to edit or improve. There are also powerful targeting options, especially Facebook, to let you have a better handle on who can see or interact with your ad. You can filter your target market based on location, company, gender, job title, age, interests, behaviors, social status, etc.

4. Generate more leads and increase conversion. Regular interaction with customers through social media and real time customer service contribute to increase in sales and customers retention. Social media is considered the most effective way to influence buying behaviour and create new business opportunities. Having a strong social media presence increases your brand's trustworthiness, making customers confident in doing business with you.

5. Improve customer service. When customers have questions or concerns, the first thing they are likely to do is look for your social media pages. Customers expect you to be on social media and they expect you to answer their concerns/problems/issues as soon as possible. Almost 70% of consumers go to social media for customer service and they want you to provide fast and round-the-clock support.

6. Increase traffic and improve rankings. Since social media has become popular, one of the obvious benefits it brought is the

increase in website traffic. It helps direct people to your website and improves your search ranking. The more popular you are on social media, the better it is for your SEO. There have been many businesses who doubt the effect of social media on SEO. But just the fact that many people are directed to your website through your social media shows how effective it is. For example, a customer who follows you on Facebook and shares your content contributes to that article's popularity.

7. Monitor your competition. One of the main uses of social media is to monitor what your competitor is up to. What promos are they doing? How are they advertising their products? What types of content are they posting? This kind of information allows you to make strategic decisions that will help you stay one step ahead of your competitors.

8. Send out messages easier and faster. Being on social media makes it easier for businesses to share content and send messages to their customers, in the fastest possible time. You can simply post an update on your social media or send direct messages to customers.

9. Cost effective. This is perhaps the most cost effective way of advertising and communicating with your clients. You can run ads on Facebook for as low as $1 per day or increase your reach by boosting posts for a few dollars.

10. Build relationships. That's why it's called social. These social media channels provide businesses and customers with a way to communicate and build relationships.
Social media has become a crucial marketing tool for businesses, regardless of size and industry. If you're not on it, then you're missing out on a lot of opportunities. According to a Linkedin study in 2014, 81% of small and medium-sized businesses (SMBs) are using social media for growth.

Social Media Numbers Every Business Should Know

- 2.3 Billion – The number of active social media users
- 1.65 Billion – The number of active mobile social accounts globally with 1 million new active mobile social users added every day. (Source: We Are Social)
- 40 million – The number of active small business pages in Facebook and 4 million of those businesses pay for social media advertising on Facebook. (Source: Forbes)
- 71% - Consumers who have had a good social media service experience with a brand are likely to recommend it to others. (Source: Ambassador)
- 91% - Of retail brands use 2 or more social media channels
- 4.4 million - Number of videos uploaded directly to Facebook in February 2016, generating over 199 billion views. (Source: ReelSEO)
- 30 % - Social media use on mobile increased by year-over-year in 2016, surpassing 2.5 billion users globally (91 percent of all social media users).

Doing Social Media The Right Way

Not everybody can run a successful marketing campaign. Remember, your social media profile is the online representative of your business. Whatever you say or post, they affect your business' reputation.

Some business owners are thinking of saving money by letting their staff handle social media. But there's a lot of reason why it wouldn't work. First, your staff were hired to do something else for your business. Second, they don't have the technical skills and know-how to run a social media marketing campaign. Third, what happens when you fire that employee or he/she resigns? You'll be left running after them, requesting access to your social media accounts. It happens a lot. Worse, if your employee left with a grudge, he or she could use your social media pages to air your dirty laundry (regardless of whether the accusations are true or not).

So, it is best for the business owner to let professional digital marketers handle their social media campaign. But you can work together with your social media manager to make sure that your social media campaigns align with your branding.

Here are some successful social media campaigns other companies could learn from.

1. Give something away if you want to get something back. Want to get new likes or gain new fans? The easiest way is to create a contest.

Mercedez Benz created a very successful Instagram competition where they hired 5 IG photographers to go behind the wheel of Mercedes CLA and whoever got the most likes get to keep the car. The campaign was so successful because the price was so big and by the end of the campaign, Mercedes got:

- 87,000,000 organic Instagram impressions
- 2,000,000 Instagram likes
- 150 new marketing assets in the form of stunning photos

Airasia also launched a campaign where participants were asked to share a snapshot of the seating plan and tag 302 friends they want to take along on a trip from Australia to Malaysia. The contest reached over 2 million people on Facebook, doubled Airasia's amount of flights and grew their Facebook fanbase by 30%.

Lesson learned: Competition is a sure fire way to attract new followers, get new likes and promote a new product. Just make sure that the prize will make the participants really interested.

2. Connect with influential individuals/brands to boost your reach. Taco Bell began conversations with Twitter users who have more than 10,000 followers to maximise the number of brand mentions, retweets and recommendations. By talking with these people who have large followings, their conversation is being read by more users. Plus, it proves that there's an actual person behind the brand.

Lesson learned: Do not underestimate the power of human touch.

3. Piggyback off trends. In the digital world where being viral is the measurement of how effective a piece of content is, it is a smart move to piggy back off these viral trends.

    The "No Make Selfie" campaign wasn't started by Cancer Research but by 18 year old Facebook user Fionna Cunningham. She asked women to post their pictures without wearing makeup for cancer awareness. People began posting and started asking Cancer Research if the campaign was theirs. Cancer Research responded by posting their own selfie and provided a number for participants to donate to. After a week, more than £8 million was raised and Cancer Research gained 826,000 Facebook likes and 140,000 Followers on Twitter.

    Lesson learned: Viral trends help you maximize your reach. But choose trends that are relevant to your business.

4. Learn how to listen. Brand monitoring allows you to know what your customers' sentiments are and in the case of Avaya, close a new deal. Through constant monitoring, Avaya was able to respond to this tweet immediately: "shoretel or avaya? Time for a new phone system very soon". This opportunity turned out to be a $250,000 sale.

   Lesson learned: Listen.

5. Create smart content and use stunning images. Social media is all about appealing to the eyes of the users. With so much content passing through their screens everyday, how can you make them pause and click your post?
   Oreo is known for their creative social media, like the Tweet they sent out during the Super Bowl when the lights went out for half an hour. The creative read: You can still dunk in the dark.

   Another brand that likes to have fun is Nutella. Their posts make you want to eat Nutella. Their stunning photos of Nutella with different ingredients and food makes people salivate.

   Lesson learned: Take quality pictures and think outside the box.

Social media is a lot of fun and offers a lot of benefits when done right. Now that you've seen all the good stuff social media has to offer, how do you start?

First, find a professional digital marketer or social media marketer who has the skills, technical know-how and industry knowledge. Next step is to create a winning social media strategy based on your goals, your competition and your budget. Then, create interesting content and post regular updates according to your social media strategy. Once you've got the hang of it, you can start monitoring and increasing your engagement for more reach. You can also do social media ads to help you get more likes or followers.

Social media marketing is more than just setting up a Page and posting updates. It takes research, creative content, out of the box ideas and an amazing strategy to make your campaign successful. Once you get it right, the benefits will outweigh your effort by not only tens but hundreds of times.

Katina Beveridge

About the author

Katina is the superwoman behind Strategic Online, a Sydney-based digital marketing agency that provides strategic digital marketing solutions to businesses of all sizes.

Building Contentcal: Starting Out, Scaling Up And Why Millennials Matter

Alex Packham

Starting a company, committing to it over many years, remaining consistent and being willing to focus your entire life towards building your business can be a truly life changing experience. From the moment I was accepted to write my chapter for this book, I wanted to ensure that whatever I used the chapter for, it had to come from a personal place so I could share my learnings.

The way I've built my company has truly changed my life, and so I want to show how if you commit to something relentlessly, it can be the same for you too.

There are 3 things I want to focus on which I think will help you build and run your business more successfully, whether you're just starting out or already running a company. These 3 things are.

1. My story in how I started out, and the importance of focus and consistency
2. How to scale your business when the time is right, and the importance of building a management team
3. Millennials and why they matter so much today

I hope you enjoy the read and take something useful away from it, no matter where you are in your entrepreneurial journey.

1. **My story in how I started out, and the importance of focus and consistency**

Let's start from the beginning. I knew I was going to build a business at 16 years old.

I just knew it was what I wanted to do. I used to sell mobile phone sim cards in the playground at my school to make money, and I was lucky that my parents taught me at a young age that if you want something, you need to work for it. The harder you work, the more you'll have.

Back then however, I was just doing whatever my parents didn't want me to do: going out late, skipping school, hanging in local parks drinking cheap drinks into the small hours. I did all those things which, as we get older, we look back on and cringe about. They are the reverse of what we thought they were; clichéd and silly as opposed to big and clever.

One thing that sustained sense in me, even during my wayward years, was my studies. I was always doing okay. Crucially, I think this has much to do with a habit of playing to my strengths – a core entrepreneurial characteristic. Hard work is often said to be key to entrepreneurial success but I would note that there is often a sort of lazy impatience in the mode of operation a lot of entrepreneurs have. We want results, and we want them now. We thrive on progress. We don't want to waste time just learning conventional, proven stuff to show we're clever. We look for the path of least resistance to whatever we want to get – not the hard way.

The fact I knew what I wanted to do at 16 meant from that very young age I was focused on being able to see the big picture for my life. Every decision I made – what A levels to take, what college to go to, which University and what course to choose – every single decision came back to the fact that one day I was going to start my own company, and I needed to map the path of least resistance to get there.

I didn't breeze my way through my education, but I've always been able to do the exact amount of work needed to get whatever grades I needed to get to move to the next level. I did this at GCSEs at high school, A-Levels at college and my skill in being able to regurgitate information that was needed to pass my exams even stood me well at University.

However for me University was not a fun experience – I found it immensely boring most of the time. In my restless search for inspiration, I stumbled upon social media marketing as a 'thing'. This was early on. The online world was another planet before 2010. It seems almost bizarre to recall. Even big companies often had a mere token presence on Facebook. Twitter was only launched in July 2006 and, until 2010, it was seen as a fashionable frivolity.

I noticed – or sensed – something shifting while I was at University; the personal and commercial use of Social Networks coming together. I was a perfect case in point myself. I was spending time browsing photos from bars Facebook pages before planning my next night out. My Newsfeed was where I'd get information about the places to go, with the best prices and the best nights; it was from a combination of business pages and friend recommendations via their status updates. The social and commercial were still separate on that feed because the big social media marketing boom was only about to hit. It seemed obvious to me that these nightclubs and bars were ahead of the game; targeting students where they killed pretty much all of their time – Facebook.

I started reading the likes of Mashable, Social Media Today and other industry blogs in an attempt to understand this nascent social community from a business perspective. I was delighted to read some wise men predicting the future as I saw it too: businesses should capitalise on this trend to reach their audiences. I could see this was going to be the future of marketing – embrace it or perish.

Later on that year, an opportunity presented itself. Or at least that is how it seems in retrospect. At the time I just had this ill-defined idea – meaning social media marketing – buzzing about my head. I was really just experimenting, with no notion of a serious job let alone a career. (Curiously, looking back it could be argued that opportunities were all around but only a few of us were lucky enough to half-notice and pick them up.)

As it happened, I was at my little cousin's 10th birthday party, a go-karting party with his mates, my aunts, uncles and family friends. It might seem hard to imagine a less likely launch pad for a career that now deals in seven digit sums. However, I would suggest that many entrepreneurs might comment; 'Yeah, that's the way these things works, ideas out of the blue and peculiar paths taken...'

After the go-karting party all the adults sat down for an evening meal and a few drinks. I mentioned to the owner of a company called Prop Store that I had noticed his company's Facebook page. Prop Store sells original movie memorabilia to film fanatics as art and collectables. I'd written coursework about Prop Store in school, college and university, partly because I am a film buff and therefore like what they do.

On their website there was a little Facebook icon linking to their page and, remarkably, this was novel enough to notice at the time. As memory serves, I think they had 99 fans on their page – at a time when fans of Facebook pages could be reached for free. Without suspecting I was about to launch my career in business, I said to the owner of the company, "I could get Prop Store a thousand likes in two weeks."

I had no idea if it was possible. I just knew this social media thing was a business 'thing', and I was determined to prove it. As I say, I had absolutely no idea it would launch the career I have today.

The owner of Prop Store invited me to submit an analysis and here, verbatim, is the follow-up pitch. It is worth re-printing in full because it catches how basic I was back then, and it also outlines the guiding principles upon which the current, gargantuan, sophisticated industry of social media marketing functions. Of course, everything is obvious in hindsight...

Hi Stephen and Dan,

I've pretty much written a mini report on the Facebook page for you because you might as well have all my opinions and then you can pick and choose between ideas you like or dislike. Either way, hopefully this is of some help to you.

Obviously I have no idea how much time and effort you have at your disposal to but I am willing to be as involved as you want/need when you have time to consider these suggestions.

Here are a few ideas to increase the exposure of Prop Store's Facebook page:-

Facebook 'fan pages' are becoming increasingly popular - enabling people to share their interests with others – and this can be exploited to the advantage of Prop Store's page. [Bizarre to think that once upon a time this needed pointing out.] Adding affiliated companies on Facebook that you are involved with from Prop Store's page – e.g. Pinewood Studios (2,388 fans) and San Diego Comic Con (11,000 fans) – Prop Store can post on their 'walls' inviting anyone to become a fan of Prop Store's Facebook page. This potentially brings more active fans to the page.

I presume that at events like Comic Con you had a lot of exposure, judging by videos on Youtube, so people who are fans of these pages may either know yourself or have heard of the company and therefore might be happy to add the Prop Store page. The Youtube channel for Prop Store has 157 subscribers with posts and comments on videos from one week ago, so it's clearly being used. If there's any way you can cross reference the subscribers on there to Facebook, so they can get more updates on Prop Store news via status updates, then that might bring more active usage!

Along with this, as I said before, movie fan pages have huge numbers of people subscribing to their status updates. You can add these pages from Prop Store's Facebook page and post on their 'walls' with information regarding Prop Store and specifically any props that are for sale from the specific movie fan page.

For example The Dark Knight has nearly 2 million fans on Facebook (http://www.facebook.com/darkknight?ref=ts), so if you wrote on the wall, briefly explaining what Prop Store does (similar to the recent Facebook posts on my page) and a link specifically to, say, the Gotham City Taxi Sign, for sale on your site, then it might attract people. Again something like Band of Brothers has nearly 200,000 fans

http://www.facebook.com/darkknight?ref=ts#!/bandofbrothers?ref=ts), some of whom are posting several times a day. You have 19 items for sale that might be of interest to these people. Of course this ploy can be applied to other pages too.

Creating an 'active' fan base:-

After fans are added, the key thing for keeping Facebook users interested is getting them to actively use the fan page and monitor activities as opposed to just being idle fans. I'm applying this theory from other companies and groups who use Facebook fan pages to interact directly with the mass of their customers (check out some of Pinewood's posts on Robin Hood and how many comments and 'likes' they receive).

A few ideas I've thought of, depending on your flexibility, are status updates from the Prop Store page stating something like "Help us reach 1000 fans! Once we reach this we will ask a movie trivia question... the first person to answer correctly will receive a $50 gift voucher for www.propstore.com!" Or, if not a gift voucher, a low value commercial prop that you don't mind giving away. This, again, depends on your flexibility and how much the page is a priority. Ideally there should be daily posts, giving fans the opportunity to interact with Prop Store and each other such that the fan page becomes a platform for communication.

Another idea is having a 'Prop of the Day' whereby a random or prioritised prop is posted on to the wall to highlight it being on the site. This would be with a view to getting people to comment or 'like' it. This may or may not do anything, just an idea to keep the posts daily. Ultimately, if you gain the image of being a 'cool' and interactive company which, at the end of the day, is what owning a noteworthy film prop is all about, then people should start interacting with your posts on Prop Store's page.

The 'Info' section on the page is currently empty. It can be filled with information regarding what the company does and that can just be copied and pasted from the homepage of the Prop Store website.

Some other suggestions:

- Potentially diversifying into a film review system, posting a short review of a new film in the 'discussion board' section on Facebook, hopefully sparking discussion from users.
- Posting links to press coverage e.g. In Loaded magazine and The One Show as they provide more commercial info on the company, rather than the specialised information that might leave casual Facebook users cold.
- Consistently asking questions via status updates on users' opinions of films, TV programmes, service from Prop Store, props

people would like to see for sale, potential improvements to services, questions about movies e.g. can you name all the James Bond films in the order they were released? Movie buffs love movie trivia – I know, I'm one of them. It might be possible to give away prizes for answers to get the ball rolling?

Once the fan base has increased then the concept of having active usage is much more applicable. None of these tasks, such as status posts, are very time consuming; they can be done several times a day, hopefully with positive outcomes.

I believe that you can reach a lot of people via Facebook and if you can be the first company selling film props that achieves a respectable presence on Facebook then it could potentially be very beneficial to your company. If you can actually get them to follow your company's actions, e.g. like tomorrow you're going to New Zealand to hang out with the makers of The Hobbit and see potential props, an update on the site saying something like The Prop Store is "Off to NZ tomorrow to hang out with producers of the Hobbit! Blah blah"...and try and think of some witty comment to include because I can't think of a clever one just now!! But just simple stuff like that should keep people interested; provide them with an insight to the company and a chance to interact with you.

Again I am willing to be as involved with the whole process as you want. As I said, it's all experience to me and it's actually pretty cool to get the chance to apply some of the rubbish I learn at Uni to a real company! If you think any of these are good ideas and want to pursue them or if you want someone to help full-time on this then count me in.

Cheers,
Alex

It all sounds so basic now but in those innocent, vanished days (of 2010 to be precise) it was impressive enough for Prop Store to hire me. I worked remotely for the company for over a year, so this email was a game changer in my life. My first proper business had taken flight after an airy comment at a ten year old boy's birthday party. And, at 19, I was soon making around £20K+ a year from my bedroom.

So at 19 – 20 I was doing this social media marketing thing and building websites for businesses, as well as running a fun media site called Cardiff Banter (think LadBible for my University, but ours was nothing compared to theirs). It was great. It funded my lifestyle, which was good for a student. It gave me financial freedom and will forever be something I look back on with great affection.

This links into the entrepreneurial lesson of this chapter. Being an entrepreneur is an attitude, it's about how you come at life. There is the obvious stuff in my journey. At school I sold simcards that I got for free from O2 on amazing PAYG deals. They fetched £10 each so I made about £100 which, at 14 years old, felt great. When I did gigs with my band I made sure we were paid whenever possible. In fact we sucked, but hey, we were bringing our friends to the venue. They bought tickets and booze, so we deserved a slice of the little pie. It followed naturally that I monetised my experience at University so I didn't have to get a 'real' job. From trying to make a fast buck and shirk real work I got a career I love.

Entrepreneurs are often slight misfits, but it's worth noting that only misfits make any difference to the world. For example I come from a happy, loving family, did well at school, was never seduced by anything untoward and can't even say I was particularly wounded in love at that time. I was just restless. Entrepreneurs are always restless. I still am today.

I'm lucky that I had found my 'calling' in life at 16. Of course I never knew if I could cut it. I only knew I had to try. In my case that meant I knew I never wanted to do the travelling thing when I graduated. For me it was already about building an incredible career in my young years. This is not a prerequisite – loads of entrepreneurs have travelled – but it is about conviction. No entrepreneur can be sure he or she will make it. And yet no entrepreneur can waste energy doubting it. You just keep going till you get there because you have always sort of done your own thing and you relish the money-making game.

So what's the point of this story? Well since graduating from University I've had two corporate social media roles, both for about 2 years each. Then, at the still young age of 23, I started my own business again. Guess what we do? Social media. Today we are 30 people with 3 offices across the globe. I've only ever worked in the industry of social and digital marketing and Prop Store is still a client of ours today, 7 years later.

If you want to be successful in business, you need to want your company to succeed more than anything else in your life. You need to **build your expertise in a narrow field, keep grinding, remain consistent and focused, and you will succeed.** From the age of 19 to 27 I've built my niche in social media marketing, and my company is one of the best in the industry today.

2. **How to scale your business when the time is right, and the importance of building management team**

Now to caveat this section, I am still well and truly learning how to scale my business. We are growing at a rapid pace, and I've only unlocked the knowledge in this section by having an amazing board of directors, some very clever investors who advise me and by having access to a group of people who support my ideas and our business.

One thing I know for sure is that you have to bring people on the journey of building a company with you. I'll never be the kind of person who thinks they can run a business with 1 leader at the top. I've been very conscious that I want to learn from people who have 'been there and done that', and can help me do what I'm trying to achieve faster. It's back to the least path of resistance concept – I need experienced people to help me get to my end goal faster.

To be able to bring investors, board members and even hire key team members, you need to show incredible passion. You need to demonstrate belief in your idea and that you will be relentless – you'll do whatever it takes to 'make it happen'.

You need to find people that will help you, and you need to understand their motive why they would want to do this. Sometimes they want to share their experience with young business people, sometimes they have made their money and want to strategically invest some of it into a new business. One of our investors tells us his investment strategy is *'back the man (or woman), back the man, back the man'*. That's how he makes his investment decisions. Some other investors scrutinize the business in immense detail as well as judging the individual. You need to understand the dynamic of this and find a way to bring these people on your journey.

This doesn't just go for investors, it goes for your management team too. No single individual can be good at everything – entrepreneurs are often amazing at turning nothing into something, often creating chaos along the way due to their constant sense of urgency. This is vital to a companies success in the early stage.

What I am learning now we are bigger, is that my sense of urgency isn't always shared by others in my management team, and their skill sets balance with mine so that we create a better business together. To give a couple of examples – we have a COO who knows how to manage a team substantially better than I ever could. We have a Director of Growth who knows how to sell software way better than I could ever deliver, and a Director of Product who knows how to build software – as opposed to me telling our developers 'just do it.' I'm still causing chaos with my sense of urgency, but it's taken through a process by these much more organised and experienced individuals to deliver a better end product.

As an entrepreneur you'll do all the different roles that a business requires to get it going. What you have to realise is that as you get bigger, you *need* help. You *need* these other skill sets to balance your team, and you need to be able to let go of some of the things someone else could do substantially better (even if you think you can do it better, trust me you cant!)

Remember a successful business is all about having an A-team. Build your A-team and your business will grow faster than you could ever image.

3. Millennials and why they matter so much today

Now this subject is often seen as a little controversial. Some people despise the fact that the word millennials is used to group a huge generation of individuals, and simply can't grasp the idea of why that generation (born in the 90s/000s) are so vastly different from the one before them.

I on the other hand am a firm believer that millennials are very different to the generations before them, and Gen Z, the next generation after this, will be different too. Here's some reasons why:

- Millennials have been told we can achieve anything in life, yet inflation increases and wage stagnation has meant that these promises simply aren't coming true for most.
- Pensions are not what they were for their parents.
- They've been priced out of the housing market till much later in life.
- They are a group of people obsessed with sharing our lives online, which has created huge social anxiety and depression in many peoples lives.
- They've have grown up with everything 'on demand' – TV, the internet, food delivery – you name it they've been able to access it almost instantly.

- At work, they come in at the bottom, but have been told having degrees and studying complex academic theories means they think they know better than their managers (which they don't in reality, something I myself learnt the hard way!)

I know some of these sound a bit depressing, but I believe they are statements that reflect the reality for so many people who are a similar age to myself.

I am in the unique position that I am a millennial CEO of a business. Our team is made up of mostly millennials. My close friends are all millennials. This I think is the most important point to make when it comes to this subject in business, is that whether you are the CEO of a one man band startup today or if you are the CEO of a corporate business with thousands of employees: *Very soon millennials and Generation Z will make up your entire workforce.*

From my own experience in the places I worked before I started my company, the clients I've worked with, and friends that run their own businesses – I can tell you now the vast majority of you are not ready for what this generation expects from their workplace.

A huge part of our success has been hiring, motivating and building a team of millennials – and I think we have done this very successfully so far.

I wanted to share some practical tips for people who are building businesses and are unsure or maybe don't understand the tactics to hire, motivate and keep this new generation.

When they enter the workplace, they learn fast, they hustle for what they want and they commit to the cause – but you have to bring them on the journey with you. They want to know why they need to do whatever job it is you're asking them to do., they can't just be told to do it with no context. It doesn't bring out the best in them.

They know companies are there to make a profit, but they don't want to see that happen in spite of every other thing a business has to offer. Businesses today can do so much to help their local communities and bring something more to the world on top of creating jobs and economic growth. Millennials want to work for companies that have values that go beyond just the numbers.

They will challenge you constantly – I get challenged by my team members who have only been in the world of work for 6 months! This group of people are not the kind that will just do something because you asked them to. I'm a firm believer in creating an environment where everyone can do their life's work, so I'm all for this kind of challenger mentality. Sometimes they are wrong, sometimes they are right. You need to strike a balance.

And onto my final point around me being a millennial CEO. Do I think there's a difference between me and some of the much more experienced mentors I've got? Absolutely. I went through the 'I know it all stage' and quickly realised through a series of many mistakes and misjudgements that I certainly do not know it all. I still go through this today and it allows me to gather learnings and knowledge that I can apply every single day.

Whether you agree with me or not about millennials, if you are a young person thinking of starting a business, there's a couple key things I wanted to share around the responsibility of being an entrepreneur and the CEO of a company at a young age:

You need to be in tune with your team as best you can be – they are the lifeblood of the company.

You need to understand what motivates different individuals.

You must be relentlessly optimistic – if you aren't, you will give up or burn out.

You need to be honest and frank – this isn't a job for people who can't give very clear and direct feedback. Every second counts.

Lastly, you do genuinely need to believe you can do anything. It might sound crazy, but I believe this of myself. I've had enough experience now that I can feel as my effort, knowledge and skills in my role get better, I get more results. I can forecast in my head how much progress we will make as a business by how much I can mentality and physically put into my job in any given week. It's a weird feeling, but incredibly powerful when you run your own company.

To be successful you need to get in tune with your own rhythm as an entrepreneur, and also learn the importance of taking breaks to re-charge your batteries when you burn out. I didn't take a proper holiday for my first 2.5 years running my own business. Sure I went abroad, but did my brain actually switch off? Not a chance. Make sure you learn how to take a break – it enables you to come back and be better than ever.

And so if you're running your own business or about to start out - good luck in your journey.

Building a business can truly change your life.

Alex Packham

About the author

Alex is the Founder & CEO of ContentCal, a marketing services and software company. The platform is used by thousands of companies across the globe to plan and publish their social media content. He started his first business at 19 years old and has worked in social media marketing his entire career. ContentCal now has 30 employees and works with some of the biggest businesses across the globe.

All Aboard: How To Keep Employees Dedicated Through Growth & Expansion

Lisa Pantelli

The greatest asset for any company will first and foremost be your employee. In today's digitally consumed society, how you treat your employee internally can have significant baring on your business reputation externally. The power of social media channels and interactive websites have created an opportunity for anyone to comment, share and like honestly and instantly.

Recruiting new candidates within any company has rapidly evolved into a process which is competitive, cost efficient and can have significant impact on the overall growth of the business. Engaging and retaining employees encourages employees to commit to *you* as an employer and the company as a place to stay and grow internally.

One of the most important skill sets an entrepreneur or manager can adopt is learning how to manage a team effectively and consistently. Understanding how to listen, trust and acknowledge their staff provides a platform for leaders to grow from; giving employees a company culture which is open, transparent and provides an opportunity to evolve within the company. It also gives employees reassurance that their voice is being heard, their work contributions add value to the company and their input into their role is appreciated.

Today, the challenge that many companies have is knowing how to keep their employees tuned in with growth and expansion; retaining their contributions and employer dedication.

The proliferation of social channels and company review based websites such as Glassdoor has created opportunities for employees to share issues that they are unhappy with as well as conducting their own research into what a company is like before they join.

In 2017, consultancy firm Edelman in their annual Edelman Trust Barometer found that trust in all four key institutions — business, government, NGOs, and media — has declined broadly and is at an all-time low. Employees are trusted more than CEOs in areas such as innovation, customer relations, crises and industry issues.

Employees are now just, if not more valuable and significant then consumers themselves. Their value and impact on a company can have devastating affects if not managed correctly and effectively.

This chapter explores the impact of employee engagement among Small and Medium Enterprises (SME's) It aims to provide you with a better understanding of what it stands for and practical tools you can use to help ensure that your business and your people have the opportunity to become the best that they can be.

What is employee engagement and why does it matter?

In 2009, as the recession was firmly taking grip of the UK's economy, Lord Mandelson, Secretary of State for the Department of Business Innovation and Skills commissioned David MacLeod and Nita Clarke to undertake an in-depth look at organisations across the UK to identify a potential link between engagement and high business performance (*Engage for Success, The Evidence, 2009*). It was hoped that by being able to prove the link between engagement approaches, it would have a 'positive impact on UK competition and performance' so that once the country had come through the recession, it would be able to meet the challenges of increasing global competition.

The findings of their research were significant. They found that businesses with highly engaged teams had:

- Doubled the net profit
- Two and a half times increased revenue
- Increased productivity
- Fewer health and safety incidences
- Better customer service ratings

The report resulted in the set-up of a Government Task Force aimed at working with UK businesses to educate and increase engagement. Subsequently, as the clear and commercial benefits were recognised between employees and business performance, CEO's have increasingly placed value in engagement and invested heavily in their people. Today, the majority of annual reports and corporate websites now dedicated a significant section valuing and crediting their employees.

A Google search will uncover many definitions of engagement. Indeed, MacLeod and Clarke identified over 50 employee engagement definitions in their Engage for Success report. A number which has more likely doubled in the last decade since it was first published!

Put simply, employee engagement: *'involves the personal commitment that an employee has to the company and its goals'* (Kevin Kruse, 2012).

What employee engagement is NOT

Employee engagement is often confused with employee satisfaction. The employee survey is often the catalyst for this confusion, as many surveys focus on satisfaction, but satisfaction itself is not engagement. Employees can be satisfied with their work, but not engaged; not willing or even able to consider putting in the extra effort to exceed.

Employee engagement is also not the quirky office furniture. Again, many businesses think that having the latest PlayStation or funkiest tables may help make people engaged. This might be creative and provide amusement, but will they stay in a job just because they can play games? The reality is highly unlikely.

> 'Customers are never going to love your business unless your employees love it first'
> – Simon Sinek

Employee Engagement and SME's

By the end of 2016, the Government released figures which highlighted that 99% of businesses in the UK are SME's with opportunity to expand and increase over the next decade.

For entrepreneurs with ambitions to grow, recruiting permanent employees is both exciting and daunting. You move from being the 'owner' of everything to needing to place trust in those that you bring on board. This is a challenge that many business owners struggle with. How do you let go parts of your business to a stranger and have faith that they will be done exactly how you would like them to be done? A crucial step if you want to keep evolving the business.

Smaller businesses can create an engaged workforce easily and effectively if managed correctly from day one. Or, if they're further down the line on their growth trajectory, they are able to be nimbler in managing through challenging times should it present itself.

With fewer processes and role positions to evolve to, a smaller group can be much easier to communicate, grow and manage making overall leadership smoother and maintainable with better visibility of their team.

Why does employee engagement matter to SME's?
<ul><li>People will play an active role in the success of your business and put in more effort to meet objectives</li><li>They will be committed to your vision and growth journey</li><li>It can reduce the cost of time taken for sickness and recruiting processes</li><li>They will act as willing advocates of your brand on and offline</li></ul>

How do you 'do' employee engagement?

Having an engaged team is not necessarily something you see or do but more something that you feel. As a business owner or a manager, you will instinctively know if your team isn't performing as well as they could be or if people are feeling unhappy.

The MacLeod and Clarke Engage for Success report identified four clear enablers of engagement. These are as follows:

1. **Strategic Narrative**: Visible, empowering leadership providing a strong strategic narrative about the company, where it's come from and where it's going.
2. **Engaging Managers**: Engaging managers who focus on their people and give them scope, treat their people as individuals and coach and stretch their people.
3. **Employee Voice**: Employee voice throughout the company, for reinforcing and challenging views, between functions and externally. Employees are seen not as the problem, rather as

central to the solution, to be involved, listened to, and invited to contribute their experience, expertise and ideas.

4. **Integrity**: The values on the wall are reflected in day to day behaviours. There is no 'say or do' gap, promises made and promises kept, or an explanation given as to why not.

Perhaps evidence as to why there is no universal definition of engagement, each business owner will, and should approach engagement differently. Each business has its own DNA; no one company is the same. The needs and drivers of employees from one sector to another are likely to be very different. Research I co-authored in 2012 *(The Science of Ingagement)* clearly identified this. We found that engineers for example, are likely to be driven by the need for integrity, meaning, experience and respect.

A common mistake made by those who are looking to 'fix' engagement is to jump in, taking a scattergun approach by changing the office layout, offering free breakfasts, or bringing in new processes in the hope of engaging their staff. While these might be nice to have, it does not necessarily engage a workforce if there is no trust between employees and leaders, for example.

They will either assume that they know what people want, or come up with ideas and possible solutions which are not focused or appropriate to meeting the root cause of the issue. This may work in the short-term but it's not sustainable and could be costly – once people expect 'free' office perks it's then hard to scale back and if engagement is an issue it won't solve high attrition levels which will also cost the business dearly.

For some practical ideas on how you can help ensure that engagement sits at the heart of your business, here are my top tips:

Tip 1: Have a clear definition of what engagement means to you

Each company is unique. This may well be one of the reasons that there is no universal definition of engagement. Start out by being clear on what engagement is for your business. Is there a definition already out there which you like and wish to adopt or do you want to have something bespoke? By being clear on what engagement is to you, will help you communicate it clearly and will affect how you put it into practice for you and your team.

This may be something you could define in collaboration with the rest of your team so that they feel part of it right from the start.

Tip 2: Clearly define what you offer and what you expect

People generally respond better to having clear guidelines noting what is expected of them. This doesn't mean a set of rules or prescriptive actions, but more around guiding principles which underpin all that they do. Some companies tie these to their values and define what behaviours are expected of the business as a whole and then by its employees. These principles can also form the basis of performance reviews.

Consider how the behaviours you display externally can apply within the business.

Tip 3: Know what you want to measure and how

If you're clear about what you want to achieve, it will make knowing what to measure much easier. This could be through a short survey, focus groups, interviews or even mapping your activity to business metrics such as reducing attrition. If you do use a survey provider, make sure that the questions are prepared effectively and you are asking the *right* questions.

Whatever the feedback mechanism is that you use, share the findings with the rest of the company and take action on the results.

Tip 4: Give people room to grow

It may be tempting when you bring on a new starter, to write out a step-by-step guide of how you do various tasks. This can certainly be a be a useful guide, but remember it is exactly that, a guide. People learn and innovate by trying new things. Give them the space to figure things out and find their own way of doing things. The more you 'tell' people what they should do, the likelihood mistakes will arise.

Tip 5: Listen and engage with your staff

Although you may have very clear ideas about what you want, the most powerful thing you can do is listen. Listen to your team and those in your immediate circle. What are they saying? Do they have ideas about how to do things differently which may save time and money? How are they feeling? Listen to what people have to say and respond. Depending on the size that you are, line managers are most likely to have a closer finger on the pulse and can help you understand what's going on. This can also help avoid any overall negative impact on the company.

You could do this by having an open-door policy so that people feel as though they can approach you at any time. Or, perhaps identify a time in the month where people can come and ask their questions.

Tip 6: Act with your employees in mind

As the owner of the business remember that you are there to lead and help your people achieve their full potential. Take on board what you're hearing and what they're telling you and look at ways of making it better for them. It doesn't have to be a monetary gesture (in fact research tells us that financial motivation is secondary to drivers such as autonomy, flexibility and collaboration) but it will demonstrate your commitment to putting the team first.

Tip 7: Communicate positively and effectively

You're undoubtedly busy but don't squirrel yourself away in an office. Talk to people about what you're doing, what your vision is and what your focus is. Share with them any potential challenges that you foresee and how important their support is to circumnavigating these.

This could be through a weekly or monthly meeting, email (although face to face is always better) or through one-to-one chats you have as you go through the office. This will instil a sense of trust and encourage a culture of openness and honesty.

Tip 8: Recruit the right 'type' of people

When times get busy it's easy to want to get people through the door quickly. Take your time to make sure you're recruiting the right type of people – not only for their knowledge and skills (both of which can be learnt) but also because of their personal values and how they would fit with the rest of the team. It's far more beneficial to recruit someone who will work in harmony with others rather than someone who knows the role but could cause unnecessary friction. Hire people who want to be there and whose energy will invigorate the team.

Warning signs to watch out for

Disengagement tends to be around moments of change such as a new leader, office relocation, redundancies and restructures, new systems or a change in strategy. As the owner or manager of the company, you will have a good sense of possible issues, but warning signs to look out for are:

- High levels of unplanned leave: people are out of the office at an unprecedented rate
- High attrition levels: people staying with the business for a significantly short period of time
- Breakdown of team work: friction between certain team members
- Lack of discretionary effort: the work is being done at a level for them to 'coast'. Little evidence of people going above and beyond to deliver.
- Poor quality work: missed deadlines, basic errors

Conclusion

There is no doubt that the absence of a universal definition can create confusion and uncertainty over what engagement is and how it should be applied, however the evidence is clear: engaged employees result in happier, more productive and more profitable businesses. At a time in which our world is rapidly changing, for SME's now is the time to think and take action and make sure that your people are ready for the journey.

SME Employee Engagement In Action: Propellernet, Making Life Better

---

Propellernet: Making Life Better

Propellernet is a marketing agency based in Brighton. They help their clients to be found online.

Their purpose is simple: To make life better for clients, their customers, their team and community. As part of this mantra, they're focused on building the best environment in the world for their people to enable them to do world-class work.

Their definition of a great place to work is an environment that cultivates growth and connection, one with a sense of pride and a culture to shout about, a place that recognises that their employees are all human.

How they make employees lives better
Their values sit at the heart of the business and they are woven into all aspects of the employee journey. Some of the ways in which this is demonstrated are as follows.

Engagement sits at the heart of the business
The business plan is focused on making their people's dreams come true. Everyone is encouraged to share what their dream is, with intent to find ways of weaving these into the business. These dreams, with the support of the business are then pursued; some have become spin off businesses in their own right or have seen people leave but in pursuit of their dream that they helped to realise.

Recruit for values, not just for skills
People are recruited based on their values to help ensure that those who come on-board are engaged with the business' culture and are willing to help take the business forward.

To help keep workloads manageable, no more than 70% of their time is billed to clients. The remaining time is allocated for agency connection, innovation, personal growth and development.

Propellernet Academy
As part of this, employees are expected and provided with the support to manage their own career development. The Propellernet Academy enables everyone, regardless of their role, to take one day a month to 'propel themselves forward' on a Propel Day. This time away from the business

enables people to innovate, create, invent and learn.

The Academy encourages creativity and curiosity. It encourages people to go out on company time and money to do things they wouldn't normally consider they could or should do at work. This can be anything from learning a new skill, language, instrument or even to drive!

The Dreamball Machine!

Perhaps one of Propellernet's most notorious approaches to engagement, as you enter their offices you are unable to miss the giant, old-fashioned sweet dispenser placed in reception. The machine is full of capsules, or rather, Dreamballs. Each Dreamball holds the name of one of the team.

Whenever they hit a target, win an award or just because they feel like it, a Dreamball is released and whoever's name is called, their dream will come true. They've sent colleagues to the World Cup in Rio, motor biking across Africa, and off to Japan for a cherry blossom season.

Clearly, Dreamballs couldn't happen in the way they do without the lifeblood of a successful business. It works because everyone has a collective sense of responsibility in seeing the business succeed and in doing so, their dreams can come true.

Maslow's hierarchy of needs is used as a blueprint to help make sure that they are meeting all the desired needs of their people. In return, they believe that they boost the economy, attract and retain top talent and do world class work.

Organisational democracy   Dream Balls   Sabbaticals   Adventures in Leftfield   Summit Days

Academy days, enhanced training, Bloomfire   Awards (for client, agency and individual achievements)   Supporting the community (inc. Make A Difference Days)   Happiness tracking and 'Big Ups'   Transparent finances   Loyalty holiday, equal bonuses

Fun and wellbeing fund (and ministers)   Weekly new news & other regular get togethers (including socials)   Enhanced induction, buddy and mentor schemes   360-degree feedback   Referral payments (for referring new or potential team members)   Hive portal   Birthday lie-in and present   Pre-payday lunch and regular bake-offs

Staff handbook   Private healthcare and a contributory pension scheme   Enhanced maternity, paternity and childcare vouchers   Safe and fun environment

Food, breakfast, tea and coffee   Subsidised massage & pilates, workstation assessments   Ride 2 Work scheme

P

Measuring making life better

The Propellernet approach has been a recipe for success. An annual survey, in partnership with Then Somehow, helps to ensure that the company and its people is operating at its best.

Their most recent results found that 82% of their team are engaged.

A survey also identifies areas for improvement. In their 2015 survey, the results found that 60% of the team *'felt good about the ways we contribute to the community'*.

With this feedback, they have since been working with two charities, the Trust for Developing Communities and the Brighton Housing Trust.

The relationship has been managed by one of their consultants who felt passionately about the rising homelessness in Brighton and he wanted to do something about it.

Within a year, the company helped to raise £30,000 and the results of the latest survey have recorded a leap to 94% of employees now feeling good about their community contribution.

The Great Places to Work scheme also provides external feedback. The company has been listed as one of the UK's top places to work for the last five years and 98% of the team would recommend working there to others.

Staff turnover is significantly lower than the industry average – 7% compared to an industry average of 30% and unplanned absences (sick days) less than five times the national average (1.1 days compared to 5.7 days).

Clients also see the benefit. Their ability to build an environment that encourages innovation, creativity, adventure, fun and wellbeing for our people translates into award-winning work for our clients.

Propellernet is hardnosed proof that being human pays off.

Lisa Pantelli

About the author

Lisa Pantelli is an award-winning founder of Become Communications, an employee engagement and communications consultancy based in Brighton, England.

Become Communications provides consultancy support to help create more productive, efficient and profitable companies. This is achieved by gathering insights and providing recommendations and strategies focused around the business' objectives.

Lisa has over 15 years' experience of working in communications and on behalf of some of the world's most successful brands including Virgin Atlantic, Discovery Networks, EDF Energy, MAC Aids Foundation, Honeywell, Sky Sports, Samsung and EY.

Lisa has co-authored a number of publications including *The Science of Ingagement* whilst holding the post of Head of Employee Engagement & Change Management at Weber Shandwick, a global communications consultancy.

She is regularly called on to judge industry awards and as a guest lecture at Bournemouth University and sits on the Inside Committee at the Chartered Institute of Public Relations (CIPR), is a member of Engage for Success and part of the employers working group for The Social Integration Commission.

Passionate about helping SME's realise their full potential, if you want to become the best that you can be, get in touch for a no-obligation consultation.

Become Communications

W: www.becomecommunications.co.uk

E: info@becomecommunications.co.uk

Twitter: @BecomeComms

Choosing The Right Finance

Adam Tavener

This subject could easily cover one whole academic year of a business studies course so, of necessity I am going to have to keep things at a basic and fairly generalised level. That said, however, this chapter will cover some simple do's and don'ts with a guide to help most new and existing business owners make better, faster choices about accessing business funding.

To me the best place to start would be to eliminate the impossible or undesirable. Your personal circumstances, track record, business plans, purpose of funding and relative affordability will all affect the availability of funding and the type that you should be seeking. Taken individually the considerations look something like this.

- **Personal circumstances.** Many lenders are happy to proceed on the basis of a personal guarantee; however they will almost always require a statement of assets and liabilities to reassure them that you can honour the guarantee if the worst comes to the worst. They will therefore consider your personal credit history, whether you are a homeowner, and if so how much equity you own. Any personal savings you have may also be relevant as well as establishing whether you have any pension assets, either personal or from a previous occupation, as these can also be used to fund your business. It is worth mentioning that if you are providing a guarantee that covers jointly owned assets such as your domestic residence a lender will also require consent from other interested parties, such as your spouse. Some time spent tidying up your personal financial profile and putting together a strong statement of assets and liabilities is always time well spent.

- **Track record.** In an existing business this is self-evident by your previous results, published accounts and so forth. In a start-up it's also important, however. Do you have any experience of the field you are entering? Can you point to a strong, relevant skill set such as sales, management or technology? Have you run businesses before? Whilst none of these things is a deal breaker, if the answer is no, they all help to build a strong overall picture of a business that is more likely to succeed.

Funders that rely heavily on personal guarantees and a credible track record are therefore likely to be inappropriate if you are not in a position to robustly address the issues above, so at this stage we could usefully eliminate them and look elsewhere.

We then need to look at the business itself, what the plan looks like, the purpose of the funding and its affordability. Starting with the business plan you should ask yourself;

- Is it credible? Did you have help from a qualified adviser when you put it together? Can you evidence your assumptions? Do you have any third party research to back up your plan? Critically, how does the cash flow and profitability projection stack up against the amount of funding you are requesting? There is no point asking for a five year term loan that will cost you four thousand pounds per month to repay if you project a thousand pounds per month of profit after eighteen months. You will immediately fail an affordability test on that basis, so would likely eliminate a loan based funding solution at that stage and look elsewhere, possibly equity.

Turning to the purpose of the funding, being clear what types of finance match your requirements will save you a great deal of time and possibly money. We tend to use the adage that you don't get a commercial mortgage to buy a photocopier, and it's perfectly true. The world of business funding is broken down into a huge array of product offerings designed to provide solutions to all sorts of different needs. In brief you might consider;

- Is the need a cash flow issue, such as seasonality or sales invoice cycles, or is it to purchase an asset or deliver a project. For the former, shorter term solutions tend to be more relevant, such as an overdraft facility or invoice discounting. With the latter a longer term solution is usually preferred, such as a term loan or Pension-led funding.
- Is there a crown debt involved which needs resolving quickly but can be repaid in the very short term, say over the next six to twelve months? If so there are plenty of short term funders who can get money to you quickly and expect it to be repaid out of near term cash flow. Not always the cheapest solution but it can be an important lifeline.

Ok, so once we have worked out what's not going to work we should be in a position to concentrate our time and energy on the line of least resistance. So let's have a look at where you might go for what type of finance. Bearing in mind that many providers offer multiple different products I am intending this to be a useful broad brush look at the scene rather than a detailed study. Some pros and cons thrown in should be helpful too. Starting with one of the most common funding solutions of all;

- Self-fund or friends and family. Lots of people have some savings put by and are willing to use these to back themselves. The clear benefit to this is that you don't have to jump through any hoops at all, and being seen to have some 'skin in the game' is seen as a positive by external funders if they are also needed. A couple of negatives, however. The scrutiny that a commercial funder will bring to the deal is a healthy sense check. Many entrepreneurs can get themselves so engrossed and passionate about their plans that they sometimes fail to ignore obvious flaws. In the event that you are self-funding it is therefore wise to go through this process with a qualified third party, lack of need for debt based backing notwithstanding. Another common error is to fail to build a formal repayment mechanism into your plans, taking the 'I'll have it back when the business can afford it' approach.

- One version of self-funding is Pension-led funding, which allows an individual with pension savings to use them as a means of financing a business. This has advantages as it is a more formal process and requires analysis of the business plan and affordability, and is therefore subject to proper rigour, however it is a regulated area and it's therefore important that the transaction is executed by an appropriately qualified and regulated practitioner.

- Friends and family. Probably the most common of all funding methods, but also the solution with the highest emotional risk factor as a failure to repay can end up with a loss of friends and a pretty uncomfortable family Christmas dinner! Joking aside, the usual mistake is to fail to make it a formal arrangement with an agreed repayment schedule and, where possible, some supporting security. The more formal you make the process the greater the likelihood of a satisfactory outcome.

Moving on to the commercial funding side of things, we need to look at the main high street offerings and also what alternative products or routes to funding exist.

- **Banks and other major lenders.** Most banks have a wide variety of funding solutions for small businesses, but it is worth noting that pretty much all of what they offer will require some form of security, whether that is based on your receivable assets, fixed assets or personal guarantee. The advantage with the major banks is that, by and large, they tend to be less expensive than many of the alternative funders; the disadvantage is that they can be painfully slow and have a very low risk appetite meaning that many early stage businesses are simply not bankable in the traditional sense. One important new initiative in the UK has recently come into play, so if a bank does decline your application for credit they must offer you the opportunity of being referred to a number of government designated alternative business funding sites which, in various ways, provide a match between your funding requirements and a whole host (up to and exceeding a hundred) of non-bank SME finance providers. For the most part this process is quick and clean, and could well provide an answer when the bank can't help. Which brings us neatly to;

- **Alternative business funding aggregator sites.** A relatively new phenomenon (think 'go compare' or 'Meer cats') these sites allow a business owner to quickly and safely enter their details and requirements. Some clever software then does a lot of background work and builds a picture of your business and the funders who would be willing to lend to you. This, in some cases, is then cross checked for suitability of purpose, so in a few seconds you can whittle down a universe of over a hundred lending products into the most appropriate four or five, and then establish contact with those funders if you so wish. Currently, in the UK there are two major players that dominate this space, Alternative Business Funding (ABF) and Funding Options.

- **Alternative online lenders.** Peer to Peer lending (P2P), where individual lenders are grouped together to provide a pool of capital to SME's, effectively cutting out the bank 'middle man' has grown tremendously over the past four years or so. Not to be mistaken with equity crowdfunding (more of that later) P2P offers some significant advantages to business owners looking for financial support. Probably the greatest of these is speed as most of these are online propositions, so if you are going to get a no you will get it pretty quickly. However, most do have telephone based support teams to manage through the more non-standard deals as well.. P2P is not a magic money tree, however, and because it is largely an algorithm based decision making process it can be pretty binary. House rules often include a minimum three years of trading, profitability and usually a personal guarantee to underpin things. It is often somewhat more expensive than the equivalent bank product.

- **Brokers.** A good commercial finance broker is a really useful asset to a small business. The best of them will be continually developing their knowledge of the market and who's offering what, and to whom. They can save a business owner time and money and rely heavily on relationships. Increasing costs and regulatory activity in the area means that many will not really look at deals of smaller value since they usually rely on a commission payment for remuneration. Historically there have been issues around professionalism and product bias which has damaged the reputation of the sector as a whole, which is a shame. Nowadays many choose to specialise in one or two areas, such as commercial mortgages, or asset finance, meaning that they are not necessarily a universal solution.

- **Start-up loans/government/local authority assistance.** There are many national or local government backed initiatives to support

SME's. The most well-known of these is the Start-up loans co, backed by the UK government. It is aimed squarely at small scale start-ups, with a maximum deal size of twenty five thousand pounds. At the time of writing I must say, however, that it is dogged with complaints of slowness, inefficiency and an overly bureaucratic approach which stifles many an application in its early stages. Local government too has a range of activities in the space, often teaming up with Community Development Finance Initiatives. Pretty much all of these have some kind of social focus and are once again targeted at micro start-ups, and are thus of limited usefulness to the more mainstream SME looking for finance.

- **Equity crowdfunding.** Another new entrant into the space, this system allows business owners (or charities, or start-ups) to list their big idea on a website where potential investors can view it and choose to back it or not, often with as little as ten pounds per investment. The sector has been dogged by controversy recently, with a number of high profile failures costing investors money. From the perspective of an SME looking for funding that really isn't a problem; however the process is not without its challenges, since, in the main, you will need to advertise your investment opportunity to the widest possible audience which, paradoxically, usually includes friends and family. Existing businesses with a large and loyal customer base usually do best since the leveraging of brand loyalty into an investment pitch isn't too much of a stretch. It is worth bearing in mind that after a successful fundraise Crowdfunded businesses tend to have an incredibly messy shareholder register which can be an impediment to further equity fundraises.

- **Pension-led funding.** As mentioned above, a derivative of the 'use your own cash' method, but delivered through a much more formal process designed to protect the value of the pension and return it a commercial level of profit. The whole thing involves an evaluation of the business, its plans and the available security. Some technical work then allows the pension (usually belonging to the business owner or owners) to grant a loan to, buy an asset from, or buy shares in the business, on a formal commercial basis. This is normally a secured transaction, but it can include soft assets such as databases, brands, and the like. The other upside is that after costs and all the interest payable is directed back into the business owners own pension. Downsides are that it's not the cheapest solution out there due to its technical nature, and it can often take six weeks or more to deliver.

- And, of course, there is always the option of taking a personal loan or remortgaging to raise the funds personally then lend on to the business. This is also a very common practice; however my warnings about a formal repayment structure stand. Do make sure you know how and when you are going to get your money out. Growing businesses tend to eat cash and without a formal structure in place you might not see your money again for a very long time.

So that's the main sources covered. A brief look at the products most commonly used and their main purposes would probably be helpful here. I have prepared the table below to cross reference product type with typical usage; however before we get into that a very brief explanation of what they are and do would be a good starting place. In no particular order they are;

- **Overdraft facility.** Normally offered by a bank, this is a flexible arrangement with a pre-set limit where you pay for what you are using at any given time. Nowadays almost always secured and reviewed annually.

- **Term loans.** These would include bank fixed term loans, most Pension-led funding type products and most P2P loans. Money is usually loaned to the business over an agreed term, often five years and on an 'amortising' basis, that is to say capital and interest are paid back in equal monthly instalments over the life of the arrangement.
- **Invoice finance.** A common way of borrowing against your receivable invoices to bring forward your cash flow. These arrangements are often 'whole book', requiring the business to effectively mortgage all of their invoices for an agreed term. In recent years new entrants in the P2P sector have developed products that allow a business to 'auction' their (usually higher value) invoices individually as needed, which brings a potential cost saving. More traditional invoice finance providers do also offer Single Invoice Finance alongside 'whole book'.
- **Asset finance.** Normally used when a business wishes to purchase a high value asset such as major plant or machinery. Interestingly there are now lots of products available which provide credit against less tangible assets such as software. Asset refinance is also frequently used where a business wishes to raise cash for other purposes and raises this cash against its existing balance sheet assets.
- **Merchant cash advance.** This is aimed only at businesses with regular credit card receipts. A merchant cash advance will assess the volume of credit card transactions over a period and offer a cash advance based on this. The funds are repaid (usually) by a fixed percentage of the future credit card takings of the business. This is normally expressed as a fee, rather than a percentage of the amount outstanding, and therefore has the advantage of putting

the risk of lower than expected card traffic (and thus slower repayment of the debt) onto the merchant cash advance supplier, not the retailer.

- **Non-bank secured lenders.** Nowadays there is any number of new style lenders who have some sort of private backing looking to lend to high quality SME propositions. These tend to be fixed term arrangements with a shorter lifecycle than a traditional bank loan, typically one to three years. The tension in this particular sector is that if you have the sort of security and affordability they usually require, then a bank may be a more attractive option for you, based solely on cost. Many have found niches that work for them, however.

- **Trade finance.** This usually comes into play when businesses are trading internationally and wish to (for instance) fund the importation of goods against a confirmed order. This product bridges the gap between paying the manufacturer, the shipping of the goods and their arrival in the UK. Often this is repaid by an invoice finance facility once the goods have been delivered to the buyer and invoiced. A specialist product but absolutely vital to international trade globally. For those businesses exporting goods abroad, an Export Finance product can be used, which works in a similar way to Trade Finance, but funds the exportation of goods against a confirmed order.

The table on the following page cross references a collection of typical business funding products against their suitability for a particular usage, where ten is the most suitable and zero the least.

This is not an exhaustive list but will cover most of the product/transaction activity commonly found in the SME sector.

Lending Products / Reason for Funding	Term Loan	Overdraft	Cash-flow loan - short term funding	Merchant Cash Advance	Invoice Finance	Single Invoice Finance	Trade Finance	Export Finance	Asset Finance	Commercial Mortgage	Performance Bonds	Grant Funding
Cashflow	3	10	10	10	10	10	10	10	7	0	0	0
Working Capital	7	10	2	7	8	10	10	10	7	4	0	0
Growth Capital	10	7	2	4	8	2	1	1	7	9	0	10
Refinance existing borrowing	7	7	0	0	7	1	1	1	8	7	0	2
Key Crucial Debts	3	8	7	8	7	0	0	0	7	3	0	1
Repay Directors Loan	8	2	2	2	7	2	0	0	7	0	0	0
Asset Purchase	8	2	2	3	2	1	0	0	10	7	0	0
Commercial Property Purchase	7	0	0	0	0	0	0	0	0	10	0	0
Business Acquisition	9	2	2	2	9	0	0	0	9	9	0	0
MBO	9	2	1	2	9	0	0	0	9	9	0	2
MBI	9	2	2	2	9	0	0	0	9	9	0	2
Purchase of Own Shares	9	2	3	2	9	0	0	0	9	9	0	0
Providing Performance Bond	2	7	1	0	4	2	0	0	0	0	10	0

Finally it is important to bear in mind that acquiring business funding is not the end of the journey. As time passes your business will (hopefully) grow and its financing needs will change. It may become more creditworthy, bringing down cost. Your existing funder may change its criteria or sector appetite; new products will almost certainly evolve which may be less expensive, onerous, or more flexible than your existing facility.

Keeping abreast of all this isn't your day job, but it is important to know where you stand since all too often finance is needed in a hurry; starting from scratch each time can be a bit of a chore and sometimes lead to a nasty shock. The new ecosystem, where aggregator sites provide not just access to funders, but also bang up to date information and the ability for you to see quickly how those funders see you is a great remedy for this.

How we all acquire funding to grow our business is changing, and technology really is making things easier and simpler. I suspect that this is how most business finance products will be distributed in the future.

Adam Tavener

About the author

Adam is founder and chairman of Clifton Asset Management Plc, the innovators behind the Pension-led funding brand (www.pensionledfunding.com), providing high quality non-bank finance to SME's across the UK. Clifton employs approximately one hundred staff in their headquarters near Bristol.

Currently more than 2,500 businesses have used Clifton for pension-led funding. With over £210million of pension-led funding provided to these SMEs, Clifton is now one of the largest alternative funding providers in the UK, and it was recognised at the Business Moneyfacts Awards 2014 as the Best Alternative Funding Provider in the UK.

Pension-led funding leverages the value of Intellectual Property (brands, logos, ideas, databases etc.) that belongs to most SME's, but which has historically been difficult to fund against.

The Clifton Group of companies also includes Pensioneer Trustee's Morgan Lloyd (www.morgan-lloyd.co.uk) and Wealth Management and Employee Benefits business, Clifton Wealth Ltd (www.clifton-wealth.com).

Adam and Clifton were the catalyst for the creation of the Alternative Business Funding (ABF) collaboration and non-bank funding portal - www.alternativebusinessfunding.co.uk. The portal unites the country's top non-bank funding providers to exchange rejected applicants for credit between themselves. In 2014, ABF successfully lobbied BIS and The Treasury to introduce legislation to force the major banks to pass over the details of rejected SME applicants to the non-bank sector.

In the course of developing the ABF collaboration Adam was part of The Treasury working group created to deliver the new bank referral legislation. As well as HMT, Adam has advised the British Business Bank, Downing Street and The Department for Business, Innovation and Skills.

Adam is a CBI regional council member.

Shine At Business – the 5-Step System to Create Your Life of Freedom and Success

Dianna Jacobsen

"When you take one step closer to your goal, the Universe moves your goal one step closer to you."
- Dianna Jacobsen

We dream of a life filled with all the things we deem wonderful, a life with all the trimmings associated with luxury and opportunity; our so-called 'perfect life'. We imagine this fantasy life, and often think that when we have
that life, then we will be successful....

But what is "freedom and success"? What does this mean to you?

For each of us this definition will be different, but all-too-often we've never taken the time to give this any thought, and to properly consider what we want to create in our lives. Generally we navigate our way through life based on the circumstances that confront us, and we're often re-routed according to the needs, opinions and agendas of others.

We wouldn't try to build a house without first having at least a mental picture – and presumably drawn-up plans – of the outcome we desire; yet we attempt to build 'the life of our dreams' without first having an image or a plan as to what that may encompass. So, too, in order to create a life of freedom and success, we must first determine what this actually means to us. This does not necessarily need to be a crystal clear vision, but a general idea or concept as to the look and feel of what we are trying to create. Don't try to define every little piece, just the overall essence. As the wonderful teacher Graeme O'Brien always said, "Into the mystery....."

So let's get started.

Step 1: Define "Freedom and Success" for yourself.

Often we associate "freedom" with having choices in life, and having options and alternatives available to us. Sometimes these choices are limited due to factors such as money or time constraints, health challenges, family responsibilities, or other commitments we feel obligated to honour.

"Success" more often is connected with our concept of accomplishment and resultant wealth; again, it is necessary to examine your personal definition of "wealth". Who is "wealthy" You? What does he or she look and feel like?

These images and feelings are critical to creating a life of "Freedom and Success", insofar as we must be that person, and feel the feelings of freedom and success in order to create that outcome.

The late Dr Wayne Dyer used to say "Don't die with your music still in you", meaning that if we have a dream, go out and create it! But first, we need to see it....

So, imagine that you have a magic wand, and that with this magic wand you can conjure up any 'life' that you desire. What would it look like? How would it feel? Who would you have around you? Where would you be? Which experiences would you like to have? What material things would you have? What job or profession would you be in? Who would you like to help along the way? Get yourself a nice little journal; this will become your personal instruction guide to life, your blueprint to "Design Your Own Big Picture". Allowing a few pages for each, use the following as page headings: Myself, Primary Relationship, Children, Family & Friends, Household, Hobbies, Finances, Business/Career, and Contribution (i.e. what you do for others). These nine headings cover all the areas of our lives.

Over time add points to the various pages describing how you'd like each aspect of your life to be. Don't worry about how this will happen, just focus on the outcome you desire. It is important to drop all limiting beliefs, so don't think about perceived obstacles such as "I'm too old / young/ broke / uneducated", or "He/she/they won't like it", or other barriers; just list the points as though you are writing a book or drawing a picture....and, really, you are! You are describing the life you are preparing to create, just as you'd plan the house you were intending to build.

Vision boards are also a great tool to use, either for your life as a whole or for specific aspects thereof, as these enable you to visualise the outcome you are seeking, and it starts to become more and more real to you, and congruent with your internal picture of yourself, the one that your sub-conscious seeks to bring to fruition. Simply find some magazines or catalogues, and collect pictures of things you'd like to acquire, and of people displaying the feelings you'd like to have. Pin these pictures up somewhere, and gradually embody these as your own. Once we can trick our subconscious into believing that we have that/ are that now, the pathways to these outcomes start to appear. The key is to be, act like, think like, feel like that person NOW, today.

Dr John Demartini says "When the voice and the vision on the inside become louder and more clear than the voices on the outside, you have truly mastered your life."

Too often, we feel that we've made a mess of our lives in the past, either in terms of money, relationships, health or whatever, and that we must untangle this mess before we can move forward. Wrong. This results in simply creating more tangle, like when we try to untangle a fishing line, or a ball of wool. The only way to truly create a life of freedom and success is to face forward, decide on our desired outcome, and take the steps needed to move in that direction. What then happens is that we disentangle past 'mistakes' around money, health, and relationships as we create the outcomes we truly seek. It's like having to turn on a light to overcome the darkness; we can't 'fix' the darkness, unless we bring in a light. Similarly with what we call mistakes. These are really just opportunities to learn, and we should be grateful for them. But they can't be fixed by getting bogged down in the problem; they can only by fixed by focusing on a solution, and working towards this. The late, great Dr Wayne Dyer said "You can't fix a problem with the same mind that created it."

In business, the primary challenges fall into four main categories: Team, Turnover, Time and Talk, meaning both the external marketing 'talk', and the internal self-talk of the business owner. So if we can encompass in our picture the outcomes we seek in all of these areas, and implement processes to manage these, we will be well on the way to living the life we dreamt of.

Step 2: Team....Build your Team, and choose a Captain

Creating a vision of the desired outcome is the same for our business. Quite often we go into business with rose-coloured glasses, thinking that we are making this decision in order to create a life of freedom and success for ourselves and our family. We imagine ourselves having the money to make the choices we want for our family and life-style, and also having the time to enjoy this.

Sadly, though, our shiny illusion is often short-lived, and the allure diminishes rapidly when we begin to realise the magnitude of obligations, compliance and after-hours work that is involved in owning and operating our own business. We suddenly see an almost insurmountable 'to do' list manifest before our eyes, and we find ourselves responsible for a whole host of 'unknown quantities', such as bookwork and taxes, staff payments, insurances, health and safety regulations, industry codes and legislation, legal considerations such as contracts and the like, financial stress, invoicing and debtor management, paying creditors on time, and so on.....

when all we wanted to do was to stop working to – allegedly – make someone else wealthy. And we completely lose sight of – and faith in – the wonderful picture we'd had.

Our newfound 'freedom' quickly becomes stressful and restrictive, and we realise that running our own business is not so much about us providing our goods or services, as it is about knowing how to run a business, including understanding all sorts of jargon and financial reports, managing staff, negotiating with various personality types in terms of suppliers, customers, financiers, contractors, advisers and so forth, and still finding time to spend with our family and friends. Our grandiose vision of 'freedom and success' can quickly disappear, and we can easily become disenchanted and experience feelings of failure and despair, if we don't have good people to guide and support us. We may even yearn for the 'good old days', of working nine-to-five for someone else, with minimal responsibility, and having weekends off...

HOWEVER......it is not that difficult to reclaim your dream, and to create the outcome you first envisaged, that life of freedom and success that you originally imagined....once you know how.

Let's start with building our team. In business, we know that we must have an accountant, and we generally need a bank manager. Sometimes we have a solicitor as well, and perhaps a financial planner (accountants and financial planners are different – they are trained and licenced to cover different aspects of your financial management, so you actually need both). We might also have someone advising us about insurance, and others guiding us with such things as superannuation, health & safety regulations or other relevant codes of practice.....and don't forget our mate at the footy/pub/butcher, or the well-meaning relatives, all giving us so-called 'sound advice' on how to run our business, and by extension, our life.

Ok, great, we have a whole team of 'advisers', some good and some not so good.....but they are each advising us from different perspectives, depending on their own viewpoint, experience and expertise, sometimes to the point of giving advice which directly conflicts with the advice from one of the others, albeit unwittingly. For instance, the role of bank managers is to structure their customers' borrowings based on equity and serviceability, whereas accountants will advise that borrowings be structured to optimise tax deductibility. It is not uncommon for these two perspectives, whilst offered with the utmost professional integrity of each party, to result in completely different loan structures, thereby being disadvantageous to the business owner from one viewpoint or another.

So what is the answer? To find one key adviser, preferably a good accountant who is a proactive, big-picture thinker, who becomes your primary adviser, and work closely with that person in managing your business decisions. Alternatively, you may choose to invest in a business coach or strategist to fill this role, however be sure to undertake some due diligence in this case, as business coaches don't necessarily need to have any professional qualifications, and may or may not have the background and expertise to fill this role of being your key adviser. Effectively you are aiming to have someone – besides yourself – casting an expert eye over the entire holistic plan on a regular basis, and connecting you with other reliable professionals as needed, covering various areas of expertise. Ideally, you want someone
with not only a business or financial background and corresponding qualifications, but someone trained in the 'soft skills' such as people management, time management, personal empowerment and well-being, as well as being conversant with peripheral aspects such as legal, marketing, staff leadership and the like. Be aware that you don't know what you don't know. They do, and their role is to fill in the gaps for you so that nothing important gets overlooked.

Step 3: Turnover....You can't fix cashflow with cash

Generally when we decide to go into business for ourselves it is because we believe we have something of value to offer our customers or clients, whether we are a tradesman, a professional, a manufacturer, a retailer, a service-provider, in hospitality, health or education, or some other offering.

Rarely do we go into business because we want to be a business manager, and deal with countless personalities, authorities, governing bodies, compliance organisations, financial institutions, taxes, staff, insurances, debtors, creditors, and so forth. However, we find ourselves meeting with accountants and bank managers, and having to take responsibility for our bookkeeping, staff wages and on-costs, taxation and other obligatory compliance.

We may or may not understand all of these numbers and reports, but it has become our duty to attend to them, and to meet assorted thresholds and deadlines imposed around them. For many people, the dealing with 'the numbers' is almost the breaking point; we are resistant, we feel stupid, we feel a sense of failure or despair, and wish we could just do what we do without having to bother with 'the numbers'. It is important to have good support when it comes to understanding your numbers. Work with your key adviser to explain and unite the various components, such as tax structure, borrowing and debt management, cashflow management, and financial planning, including superannuation, wealth creation, investments and insurances. Have your chosen adviser explain to you, in simple terms, how your financial results are currently being generated, and what your financial reports mean, relative to your day-to-day actions within your business. Have this person support you in establishing systems for managing your finances, and, if necessary, in conversations with lenders and other parties regarding your money management. Engage a good bookkeeper to handle your data input and to produce reports from which you can monitor the daily / weekly
/ monthly performance of your business.

Most business owners find themselves struggling with cashflow at some point in their entrepreneurial journey, and their first inclination is to increase borrowings, restrict spending and consider down-sizing; anything to save money. And while this concept has merit up to a point, you can't expand a business with a mindset focused on contraction. Of course, you must work with your accountant to determine appropriate pricing and margins, as well as tax rates and other relevant management decisions;

and review your Input costs including things like insurances, telephone, and advertising. But besides addressing the obvious leakages, the key is to enhance the business' top-line, the gross turn-over.

Conversely, I'm sure we all know of people who have had a large cash injection from some source, only to find themselves back in the same financially-challenged situation soon after. This is because the systems around the money management are not sound, and also because their mindset is not congruent with their new or desired level of wealth. Hence the philosophy that you can't fix cashflow with cash. Rather, this is done by looking not just at the Profit & Loss Statement, but outside it, at the aspects that create the cashflow.

Picture your Profit & Loss Statement, or perhaps your Bank Statement. Either way, we are interested in the bottom line, the one showing how well we've done for that period, like a school report card. However, we must consider the system, and all the other aspects that impact on CASHFLOW, and on that bottom-line balance, and which are, in turn, impacted by it; things like our TIME usage, our MARKETING, our STAFF, and the cost of our INPUTS. But then, think further: our business results are equally impacted by, and have impact upon, our HEALTH, our RELATIONSHIPS, our FAMILY, and our LIFE BALANCE, any of which can have a significant negative impact upon our business' well-being in the event of a personal problem or health challenge.

If a business is experiencing cashflow shortage, and the obvious issues around the cost of INPUTS (pricing, expenses, margins, etc.) have been addressed, put a short-term cash management strategy in place, by negotiating payment plans with creditors, so you can concentrate on building your business. Begin by reviewing the use of your TIME (are you focusing on your cashflow drivers?), implementing an effective MARKETING plan (who is your audience, and what outcomes do they seek?); and reviewing your STAFF leadership and management (have you assessed the strengths of your team, and customised their roles accordingly?).

It is also important to check in with your personal well-being, in terms of your HEALTH, RELATIONSHIPS, FAMILY, and LIFE BALANCE, because a business, as an extension of its owner/manager, cannot operate at optimum level if you are distracted by personal problems or sub-optimal health. When designing your 'dream' outcomes, it is important to include your sense of personal well-being and life balance. These eight factors are the critical elements to generating a healthy cashflow, work-life balance, and creating and living a life of true freedom and success.

Step 4: Time....to Shine.....and to work, rest and play

One of the most common complaints of business owners is the lack of time, and the never-ending list of things to do, which becomes overwhelming and insurmountable. We feel that we need to work harder and harder, longer and longer hours, and that when we get caught up, we'll be ok. But we will never get caught up, because more and more tasks add to the list daily. This phenomenon is exacerbated by the fact that small business owners are often
'solo-preneurs', trying to be all things to all people, and to save a few dollars wherever we can by performing all manner of tasks ourselves, personally. This sense of overload and overwhelm can lead to health problems, and relationship rifts, which in turn add to the sense of despair and fatigue.....a seemingly endless treadmill which the business owner can't step off. There is a solution, however.

As we said earlier, we generally go into business because we have a skill or product to offer the world; if we are a skilled service-provider or professional, then we, personally, will be performing that service or delivering that skill or expertise as the client is paying for us, and for our time. However, if we are offering a product or more generic style of service, such as retail or hospitality, it won't necessarily need to be us, personally, who undertakes the delivery, rather the customer is paying for an outcome, or for a product.

Either way, there is a large part of the process that does NOT need to be performed by us, the business owner, in person: tasks like collecting the mail, sweeping the front path, ordering the supplies, attending to the bookkeeping, doing the cleaning, answering the phone at reception, and so on and so forth. We think that if we undertake all of these simple tasks, we will save ourselves money; but all we are really doing is replacing our chargeable time with lower-level time-fillers and busy-ness. We are sacrificing time that could be spent concentrating on our cash-flow 'drivers' – i.e. the tasks that generate our cash flow, whatever it is that we write invoices for – in order to save $10 or $20 per hour on more generic tasks that could easily be delegated or outsourced. These numbers are not difficult to do.

The objection to engaging someone else to undertake these lower-level tasks usually lies once more around cashflow. However, there is a specific sequence that will enable this transition to work effectively and efficiently. Firstly, as the business owner, identify your core cashflow drivers, being the tasks from which your business derives income; this list should include Marketing and Management. Next, list all of the other things that take up your time: mail, banking, bookkeeping, cleaning, filing, lawn-mowing, housework, ironing, shopping, driving, phone-answering, etc...... Beginning with the more obvious tasks that are easily delegated, such as bookkeeping or cleaning, off-loan one task per month to a suitable recipient, and the time you have just 'bought' for yourself should be utilised effectively, such as with billable time, or promotional activities, to cover the cost of the task outsourced or provide leverage toward future income.

By delegating out one task at a time, you are able to work to your strengths and skill-sets, and thereby spend more of your time undertaking cash-generating tasks and building up your top-line, rather than restricting and reducing your business. We humans also tend to have more enthusiasm and energy when we are performing tasks which we enjoy, whereas tasks we don't enjoy drain our energy and leave us feeling fatigued and resentful; so find someone who does like to do those activities, and let each person work to their strengths.

Additionally, be sure to make time for the things that are truly important in life, such as your personal health and well-being, and time spent with loved ones. Too often, business owners feel that time spent not working is unproductive time, but this logic is flawed; what is the point of working and creating money and choices, if not to achieve a balanced and fulfilling life, in all aspects? By having written in your "Design Your Own Big Picture" journal, you will have identified the core priorities in your life, and from this, you can make choices around how you spend your time as well. Simply make decisions that move you towards the desired outcomes you have set for yourself, and decline the options or distractions – both in terms of time and money – that may sound good, but aren't aligned with the direction you have chosen; bear in mind, though, that there will always be exceptions when
'shiny' opportunities arise, and you can mindfully consider whether or not you will take that diversion or not; either way, your decision has been made with awareness and empowerment.

Step 5: Talk.....Watch what you say, inside and out

No matter what we may believe, it has been proven again and again, that how we think, speak and act has a measurable impact on the results we manifest. Accordingly, then, it is critical that we not only think, speak and act positively in terms of our marketing spiels and promotional or networking verbiage, but that we also remain empowered and optimistic within ourselves, so as to maintain optimal outcomes in terms of our own frame of mind, as well as in our interactions with staff, customers and suppliers, plus keep an overall and over-arching belief in reaching the goals we have set for ourselves.

We are inundated daily with advertising propaganda, marketing spiels and promotional offers from the outside world, all promising wonderful results to be gained from purchasing the vendor's goods or services.....clearly this is the role of marketing as a whole, to sell the end-user on the outcomes they will enjoy by purchasing this widget.

But what about our own, secret, inside voice, the one that wakes us at 4am to worry about the bank balance, or the staff issue, or the payments due, or the delivery that is late....? While the external marketing talk has an obvious impact on the well-being of a business, this internal talk of the business
owner can have catastrophic effects, not just on our personal health and well-being, but on everyone around us, like the ripple effect of a stone thrown into a pond.... because, as the leader, the morale of the business owner permeates the entire business, and those who encounter him or her will sense, if not directly notice, the undercurrent of negativity, and feel less attracted to that person or that business, often without even knowing why.

This is where it is imperative that we, as the business owner, turn again to our team for support, guidance and encouragement. The journey of an entrepreneur can be quite lonely at times, leaving the business owner feeling isolated and discouraged. By operating with a team, it becomes much more of a collaborative process, and the burden is shared and managed much more effectively, and with considerably less personal 'damage' in terms of stress and despair, and less damage to the business from the negative 'vibes' which others sense. So while the marketing talk is definitely important, the self-talk is crucial.

In terms of a marketing plan, this need not be costly and time-consuming. Despite the many options available these days to advertise a business, it is best to choose a maximum of four or five strategies, each with a few tactical steps to implement, and stick to this consistently, rather than taking the
'scatter-gun' approach, whereby a business tries a bit of everything, and nothing really works.

To enact an effective marketing plan, first get clear on your target audience. Next consider where they seek their   information: is it online, in the newspaper, on Facebook, industry journals, networking events, or elsewhere? Once you have some understanding of where they are looking, reading and shopping, design your message accordingly, using language and keywords that will resonate with that audience. A couple of effective strategies may be: attending selected relevant networking events and connecting with either your target audience or people you can collaborate with; having your Facebook page well-presented and feeding into your website, which offers an opt-in to receive your newsletter or similar, and following-up with an appropriate email introduction; forming Joint Ventures with complementary businesses so you can collaborate to bring a package deal or value-add offer to their clients as well as your own; encouraging word-of-mouth referrals from past or current clients, perhaps with a bonus offer to reward them for their loyalty; writing for a local publication about your area of expertise with a view to giving insight and value to the reader. Other than needing a website, these strategies can all be done for no cost, but are among the most effective methods to promote various types of business.

By working through these broad steps, and implementing simple strategies within these areas, that life of freedom and success that you day-dreamed about is not so far out of reach as you may have previously believed. Give some consideration to what that ideal life might involve for you, how it may look and feel, in all aspects of life. Define what 'freedom' and 'success' really mean to you, and set some goals to move towards.

To have a business that truly shines, learn to understand the numbers, of course, but pay close attention to all the components that generate the numbers. The Profit & Loss Statement and your Bank Statement are merely scorecards showing your results to date, and these do not have to be predictive of your results in future.

The future is in your hands, and in the use of your TIME, MARKETING, and STAFF leadership, all of which can be managed easily with appropriate strategies and sequences in place, supported by your team. Concurrently, give due attention to your HEALTH, RELATIONSHIPS, FAMILY and LIFE BALANCE, as these have just as big an impact on the resultant productivity and profitability, particularly when they are overlooked or mismanaged.

Take heart, and feel empowered: you can control the numbers, by understanding and managing your Team, Turnover, Time, and Talk, and you can create a life of freedom and success by learning to love your life right now, and to Shine At Business!

Dianna Jacobsen

About the author

Dianna Jacobsen grew up in southern NSW, Australia, on her family's wheat and sheep farm.

Having seen small businesses and rural families struggle, Dianna chose to enter the field of accounting and business advisory services after finishing school, with a goal of making a difference to these people, and has now spent almost 30 years working with families and small businesses to help them create lives of freedom and success, in terms of personal and financial well-being and empowerment.

In 2005 Dianna sold her public accountancy and taxation practice, having identified a raft of small-business advisory needs which were not readily available. Having founded Shine At Business, Dianna now specialises in bringing together all aspects of business development and financial strategic planning in a holistic, integrated approach, including day-to-day money management, staff leadership, marketing, life balance, goal-setting, debt structuring, legal considerations, wealth creation, business psychology, succession planning, and time management. She works with families and business owners locally and interstate, and holds a role nationally as the Australian financial strategist for Loral Langemeier's global Live Out Loud community.

Combining her various qualifications including accounting, financial planning, small business management, and personal empowerment coaching, Dianna assists businesses, families and individuals across Australia to guide them to creating their lives of freedom and success. Having experienced various chapters in her own life as a business owner, a mother, a cattle grazier, a conference speaker, and mostly as a busy woman juggling assorted roles, Dianna works with people to identify their individual and specific needs, and then supports them to implement a customised and realistic action plan to achieve their goals.

Dianna also writes regularly for a number of publications and websites, appears in various media as a guest expert contributor on topics covering a broad range of financial, small business management and personal empowerment issues, and hosts a local radio program. She speaks regularly at conferences and conducts workshops, seminars and webinars. She has been featured in assorted publications, including The Motivational Speakers Handbook of Australia.

Making Things Happen

Orsolya Bartalis

I read somewhere the other day that people are braving entrepreneurship instead of taking on jobs that don't inspire them. I feel that is a great decision. If you have not always been an entrepreneur however, it can be a hard and scary decision to make. Why? Because most of us have the training of an 'employee'.

What do I mean by that? Unless you had parents that were entrepreneurs themselves, the message of the century was 'work hard, get good grades, and get a good paying job'.

In my career, I have seen time and time again people feeling stuck in their current position due to the fear of what the change may bring. Failure, success, looking stupid and not meeting others' expectations are the most common fears that I have seen holding people back from making the jump and become an entrepreneur.

And for those that have jumped, the retraining begins. Why? Because if you have an 'employee' mindset as an entrepreneur you will burn out. According to the Australian tax office, you will work harder than ever and earn peanuts. This is not what entrepreneurship is about.

I wasn't always an entrepreneur myself, however I found that my journey from an employee to an entrepreneur is not unique. As I now help others to create their exit plan from high demand corporate roles into entrepreneurship, I found that the fears, blockages and limitations are the same as mine, even though our stories are different. So let's look at what we need to break through to make sure we make things happen.

Major Show Stopper - Unworthiness

I found that the mindset blockages that we have to overcome actually turn up as patterns in our life. Unless you stopped, looked back and analysed each of the situations that were challenging you along the way, you would not have noticed the connection. Maybe it is time you did so. Amazing what you will find!

Unworthiness is something you may not even identify with. The reason for that is that unworthiness doesn't mean that you have low self-esteem. It doesn't mean you are not successful. And it doesn't mean that you are a shy introvert. It is however the underlying cause for you not breaking through that silver lining or self-sabotaging yourself as soon as you are about to achieve something amazingly great!

Do you remember being punished as a child? Whether it was for failing, being wrong or perceived to be naughty? What is the feeling that is coming up now as you are thinking about such an incident? Most of us didn't have the emotional intelligence back then to separate our actions from ourselves, as such the conclusion is generally a negative one for such event.

Instead the thoughts would have revolved around 'I'm bad', 'It's all my fault'. Every time there is such an incident we re-confirm these messages. Over time the generalised link becomes 'I'm not worthy'.

Two things generally come of this; one is that the person becomes an 'under achiever' doing anything possible to confirm this notion. The other is that the person tries to undo the feeling of unworthiness and becomes an 'over achiever' proving whoever hurt them they were wrong!

The latter goes and achieves many things, but not of their own accord. It generally starts with a 'bet you CAN'T do this!' These achievements are hollow and endless, because no amount of success will make any difference to how we feel inside.

In either case, the lesson we need to learn is that we are not the things we do. Looking at success or the lack there of, based on an outside-in process will mean that we will never find satisfaction and fulfilment no matter what we do. Instead we will feel empty inside.

The feeling of unworthiness can also be brought up if you were bullied. 'Too fat', 'Too short', 'Too old' are again not who you are. And, very often, these beliefs we have of ourselves come from other people's comments. So do yourself a favour and check if you even identify with any of the negative comments you may have received or if you have just taken on someone else's perception of you as your own belief.

We tell these stories to ourselves about why we are unworthy based on our beliefs, things that we have done but didn't feel accepted for and our thoughts that we linked to these events, or rather the memory of such events. However we need to let go of these. You are none of them! Once you can look beyond these you will find who you really are. Let's call it your higher self. This self is perfect, loveable and amazing. It has all the knowledge within that you need to get ahead in life.

When you can connect with your higher self, every goal, target action will come easily. You will also find fulfilment and satisfaction in life. Whilst you are trying to please others – or prove them wrong, you will always feel less than what you really are.

What you focus on becomes your reality

I have had the privilege to meet several people that have cured 'themselves' of cancer after the medical team has told them they only had a short time to live. They may have had some medical help, but with that sort of diagnosis the biggest difference in the outcome they attribute to their mindset. They refused to give up!

Lucky for me, my health was never affected to such levels, however my bank account sure was! When I looked at it with my newfound awareness I found that I was well versed in poverty! The lessons I got growing up were around:
'Work hard to get ahead', 'whoever has the money, is in charge', 'money doesn't grow on trees', 'unless you were born rich, you will not get ahead' and the likes. No wonder I was repelling money!   Although I didn't necessarily hold these comments to be true, I have heard them since birth, as such my subconscious mind was programmed to be struggling to build wealth.

Unfortunately for most of us, our original programming happens before you can do anything about it. It has been proven that these programs are set by the age of 7! Which is a scary thought really, since our mind is great at bringing to us the people and events that we most powerfully focus on. I say powerfully because these programs are running in our subconscious, and until we become aware of them and change them they can run without us even realising. With 50,000 thoughts running in our heads each day, it can be hard to keep up.

So I mentioned the subconscious mind. This is the beast you need to conquer! This is the part of your mind that will make you self-sabotage in oh so many ways. This part of your brain has the language of your senses – smell, feelings, images, sounds, tastes and touch. It takes up about 50-60% of your entire brain capacity. You know that 'gut feeling' you get? It comes from this part of your brain.

The subconscious brain works with the conscious brain, which is the part that thinks, acts and talks with us. Together these two will deliver what we focus on. So for me, it delivered a lack of money in the bank, even when I was making a lot of money, due to my programming.

Lucky for us, if we don't like our programming we can change it! Firstly you need to become aware of your programming around life, money, relationships and whatever else you feel isn't quite up to the standard you want to have.

I suggest you do each area separately. Pull out a piece of paper and start writing your thoughts down. Put some time aside and let the thoughts come. Then look at which ones are propelling you forward, and which ones are holding you back. The ones that are holding you back need to be turned into a positive affirmation.

Say for me it was 'I have to work hard for my money'. I turned this into 'I do what I love, providing value and attract abundance by doing so'. You will need to practice the new affirmation daily, until it becomes second nature to knock out your limiting belief.

Beware however that the affirmation needs to be in a language that your brain can accept. Also make sure it is in a positive language, as your subconscious cuts out things like 'don't' or 'can't'. So if you affirm 'I don't want to be poor', guess what you are going to get?

Also make sure it is in the present tense, it cannot be in the future as you will never achieve what you are aiming for.

Basic Mind Laws

1. What you resist persists – meaning that what you fight against will ensure its persistence. The easiest way to describe this is when we say 'I don't want to be like my mother'. The more you reinforce this the sooner you will find that you are just like your mother.

The easiest thing to do is to acknowledge the existence of what you are resisting. Don't fight it, instead deflect it.

So in case of the above example, you need to say 'She is what she is. She did her best despite her shortcomings. I choose to let go of her limitations and become successful in my own right'.

2. What you sow you shall reap – This saying has been around thousands of years, and really is timeless. What you have to realise is that what you put out may not always come back from where you expect it from. I find this with money all the time.   Also it comes back at a higher volume than what you give, so be very careful to not give out negative vibes!

3. Commitment - You cannot decide to be an entrepreneur half- heartedly. That will give you very ad hoc results! Once you commit to whatever you choose to do whole-heartedly, your success will go through the roof. And when it comes to entrepreneurship, I found that if you cut out the possibility to go back to a job, your chances of succeeding double.

4.Be challenged, but know your why – Have you found that as soon as you set a goal you are ready to procrastinate? To get things off the ground you will need to put energy in. Lots of it! If you have a strong reason you went into business to start with this will come naturally. If you are wondering what it was all about, it will mean some soul searching.

Questions like – Is this something I really want to do for the rest of my life? -is a good start. Would I still do this if I wasn't paid? Is this venture fitting in with my life/family and other plans? How is this adding value to the world? Am I contributing to society?

To me being an entrepreneur is like a personal development course on steroids, you learn so much. So the challenge will always be there. The question is, do I have a strong enough reason to keep going? If the answer is positive to that question, you will be driven to make things happen.

5. Need to understand before you bust a blockage – It is well and good, you no longer want to be broke. But first we need to understand what it is we got out of being broke in the first instance to break through the blockage, not just stop overspending. You may be able to conquer overspending, but find that you now have an eating disorder. Did I mention everything happens in a pattern till you solve what the real issue is? You need to master these laws and implement them to become the master of you.

Success Secret: Goals

I love the saying 'Goals in writing are dreams with deadlines'. That is only the first part, declaring them openly will get you even better results.

Goals are something that are in common knowledge, yet I find so many people still being confused about how to set them in a way that are driving them forward to actually achieving them.

First mistake I find is that people are not willing to commit to their goals in writing. 'It's in my head' – I hear that a lot. Anyone can sit and consider what they want to happen, only people that really want to make things happen will commit to it on paper. So if you haven't already done so, make sure you get your goals out onto paper after this chapter! This action actually mobilises your brain to make the goal happen.

Let me put a different take on a goal. The real purpose of a properly set goal is not to achieve the target, but to give you motion and help you develop as a person along the way to achieving your goal. The goal may even change over time, but if you do not have one to start with, how will you know if you are even on the right path?

But what if I fail? You may ask. We do not fail well in our society due to programming. We learnt that failing is a bad thing. However failure is a great thing. It teaches us what didn't work and what we need to change. That is if we are ready to learn from our failures along the way to reaching or goals.

A surprise may be that a fear of success is just as strong - if not stronger - as the fear of failure that holds people back from setting goals and achieving them. Why? Success means change, it means that we will be on an unfamiliar territory outside our comfort zone. It means that we have to live up to our own standards and expectations.

Once you break through these fears you need to be able to set your goals based on what is important to you, what you value most. Is it freedom? Family? Security? What is it that you want to have in your life as a must?

If you want security, then entrepreneurship may be hard, depending on what your definition of security is. If it is regular pay check, you will have a major conflict possibly, as entrepreneurs – especially in the beginning – will have various pay checks. So be careful what you choose.

You need to use these values as the filters when you make decisions going forward, as if there is a clash with them, you will bring unease to yourself.

Now you can set your goals. Business and personal life can be a little blurred when you are an entrepreneur, so best to set your goals for each of the roles you play. Being entrepreneur, partner, mother/father, son/daughter etc.

When you are ready to set the goals, there are simple rules:

• Make them Specific

• Make them Measurable – exact figures, deadlines and the likes, help. What gets measured gets improved.

• Make them Achievable yet challenging – too easy won't help you grow! But don't make them to be so far out of reach that your mind cannot believe that you can achieve them.

• Make them Time Bound – simple caution here. People tend to overestimate what they can achieve in 12 months and underestimate what they can achieve in 5 years.

• Review constantly and celebrate – this is an important step. Seeing your progress and celebrating the positive action reinforces more positive action to make things happen. Yes, you are worth it! Yes, you have done a great job! Better believe it.

Make things happen

Have you heard about the 4 minute mile? For years people were unable to beat the record for running 1 mile in 4 minutes. Roger Banister broke this record. Once he did there was a flow of people that broke his record, because once he has done so, they had proof that it could be done.

What Banister did was practice in his mind breaking that record. He planted that program into his subconscious. You can do the same. There are different ways of doing it. I recommend to practice rehearsing this at the time you practice gratitude, and preferably that is to be at the same time that you exercise. The reason is because in that state, you are at a heightened level of emotional awareness.

The steps are as follows:

1.   Start exercising, once you warm up and feeling positive think about the things you are grateful for. Everything you have in your life now.
2.   If you can say it out loud 'I am grateful for having financial freedom'
3.   Notice the feeling that goes with it
4.   After saying several affirmations for things that you are grateful for and have already achieved, say 'I am grateful for this goal, I achieved' – say it in presence tense, like you've already got it even though it is something you are working toward.
5.   Keep it going for at least 5 minutes, preferably in the morning.

The reason I recommend to voice/visualise your goals while you express gratitude is because it will help you link a positive emotion to them, and it helps your subconscious to get hold of your goals and make them a reality.

Make sure you add plenty of positive emotion! Emotions add tremendous power to propelling you to achieve your results. And then repeat! Repetition is the key to implementing new programs.

The other thing we have to remember to make things happen is not to let our circumstances now define our outcome for our future. Just like the time I hit rock bottom, working hard, long hours barely breaking even. I had the choice to either feel beaten, or say 'this is not on! I need to change my reality'. I chose the latter.

So when things are not going well in your life, which outcome will you choose?

Why do we procrastinate?

You worked through your negative emotions, beliefs and have set your goals and know why you want to make things happen. So why is it then that you still find yourself procrastinating, leaving things to the last minute or not doing things that would move you forward. Sounds familiar?

What we have to look at when we find ourselves procrastinating is what we get out of not taking action? If you have a hint of perfectionism, then you may find that the message is that there is no point in starting things till everything lines up perfectly to make things happen. Or it may actually be the 'what if I try and fail' scenario that is holding you back from starting.

Like I mentioned we tend to look at failure as a negative, as such we take it rather personally, and come to the conclusion that we are not good enough if we fail. So why would you want to start something that will possibly lead you to the confirmation of such?

But what if you looked at failure as a learning experience? Your outlook to get things started would be much different. Many people failed their way to success. Look at Donald Trump who was bankrupt before he made it big in real estate. Or Thomas Edison who proclaimed that it took 9,999 failures to get the light bulb right. Or even you, learning to walk, to talk, to write, to drive. You didn't get them the first time you tried either.

Unfortunately as we grow up we get trained to be risk averse. But giving something your best shot is the only way to build resilience, courage and the positive affirmation to yourself that you can do what you set out to do. Embrace the challenge, moving forward is not as scary as the fear makes it out to be.

As you move forward despite the fear that you may have, you could find yourself facing self-sabotage. To get consistent results you will need to accept the flow of abundance. It doesn't matter whether it is in the form of health, wealth or happiness. We all have our internal limitations that we need to break through.

Tony Robbins explained this phenomenon with his business. He found it easy to make his first million dollars, but then took him years to break through that limit, because he was not comfortable with receiving it.

When we are not comfortable we will do anything to make it go away. Just look at lottery winners. Several studies looked at the effect winning the jackpot had on some people. They found that some winners were eventually left worse off in debt, with a trail of broken relationships behind them.

So let's get comfortable with accepting abundance. You can have happiness, health and wealth to the levels you desire. To move forward rationalise with yourself that the wrong move can be corrected. In fact sometimes what we think is the wrong move is actually the best move!

Make your decision a positive emotion. Instead of saying how much you hate a certain task that you need to do, think of the positive outcome you will get for getting it done. It's like going to the gym, you don't tell yourself how tiring and painful it will be! You look at that healthy fit body that you will get in return.

Once you get going, you may become aware of the impulses that drive your actions at times. Making your actions ad hoc and finding that you aren't making the decisions you should do. This is where you will have to insert the GAP.

Enter the GAP

The first I heard of the gap was from Tony Robbins. I thought it was an interesting concept as implementing it helped me realise how many things

I was doing on impulse, based on an emotion, that were not supporting me.

Have you ever found yourself walking to the fridge, not even being hungry, just to find that your hand went in there and found that piece of chocolate cake that you didn't want to eat? Cake is not the only thing that can suddenly appear, it can be the latest gadget, the 10th pair of shoes or the Gucci bag.

So next time you are about to act on impulse, stop for a moment – it will require your awareness of the situation in the first instance – and insert the GAP. This can be in different forms, depending on the impulsive action you are taking. If it is eating, I normally suggest you drink a glass of water and contemplate whether you are actually hungry or covering up some negative emotion with food. Discover what the real reason behind your action is.

The GAP allows us to use our emotional intelligence by preventing an automatic action. At times this requires you to slow down and really discover what is going on. I hope you have noticed by now that making things happen has a lot to do with our emotions, thoughts and beliefs. In fact they are the driving force behind everything we do. What we can see on the surface is just the story we bought into about ourselves through our life.

We beat ourselves up for things we did or didn't do, and hold onto them for years. Because of this we won't accept ourselves lovingly, or give ourselves another go, through this we build our negative programs. These can take years to build, don't expect that undoing them will happen overnight.

You will need to be patient with yourself. Commit to utilising the tools above, and learning more about yourself. Deep wounds may need to be brought up to the surface so you can deal with them and break through the limitations they caused. If we don't deal with the deep-seated issues, they will keep on returning in the face of different challenges till we get it. Start today.

Orsolya Bartalis

About the author

Orsolya knows the power of setting her intentions and achieving goals. At the age of 16 she set out to move to Australia and was there within 12 months. Since her time here she has travelled around, learnt about various industries, and enjoyed a great career in HR.

Before becoming a Success Coach Orsolya found herself being a single mum, working long hours, yet barely making ends meet. This is when an opportunity came along to work away, four weeks at a time. Whilst this was great to help Orsolya clean up her debt, it came with the sacrifice of not seeing her children.

This is when Orsolya decided that something had to change! She set an exit plan to become financially free and do what she loved the most – help people become the best version of themselves. This meant that Orsolya had to bust through several blockages when it came to her belief around money, work and herself.

She is now enjoying the financial freedom and doing what she loves, so Orsolya decided to help others to devise their exit plan, and set a goal to inspire 10,000 people to create their dream life.

And Finally...Top Tips To Manage Your Cashflow

Gary Turner

Cashflow management is what separates good small business owners from great ones. While it may not be as exciting as making a big sale or scoring a round of financing, managing the cash coming in and out carefully provides a definite business advantage. Having enough cash to meet outgoings is critical to small business survival and long-term sustainability.

Most businesses start with a small amount of cash and as revenues grow, they have enough money in the bank to cover the bills. Problems arise if the money coming in doesn't cover operating expenses. This may come about simply because customers are slow to pay – or when the business needs to make a large purchase, take on a loan, hire an employee or offer credit to customers.

Cashflow management can make or break a business

Just 41% of UK companies survive the first five years – and cashflow is crucial. Research by Xero into what separates successful entrepreneurs from those who fail revealed that:
- successful small businesses keep their finances in order
- money is the lifeline of small businesses, and cashflow is the single biggest factor and contributor to their success or failure
- 65% of failures blamed financial issues like cashflow visibility and access to capital
- 58% of survivors use software to manage their finances compared to only 14% of failed businesses

These insights came out of the Make or Break report which examined the experiences and attitudes of over 2,000 current and former small business owners from the UK and USA. It sought to uncover the small things that make a big difference to entrepreneurial success.

Managing your finances and cashflow
You can take some simple, practical steps to help control spending and grow your business without taking excessive financial risks. They involve:

- knowing your numbers – have a clear picture of your business finances
- invoicing promptly and accurately – encourage your customers to pay on time and regularly
- getting paid fast – benefit from more cash in your account
- using cloud accounting software – simplify managing your business finances

Knowing your numbers

To be a successful entrepreneur, you need to know where your cash comes from and where it's spent. These are the numbers that drive your business. They're what you need to know to keep your company running day-to-day and to grow it when the time is right. It's vital to keep your books accurate and up-to-date so you can see the financial state of your business at a glance. Here are some tips:

Keep your business and your personal finances separate

The easiest way to keep your business and personal finances separate is to have separate bank accounts and credit cards – and to use the right one for the right things. Then you'll be able to see how much cash your business is generating.

Let technology work for you

•   Online accounting software automates key tasks and processes, which helps you save time and keeps you compliant. Software that automatically imports your bank statements each day and makes it quick and easy to reconcile them means you have the latest information any time you need it.

•   Technology helps you understand the numbers. Smart accounting software makes it easy to plan, forecast, track and chase your company's money. It provides the information and insight you need to steer your business in the right direction. With online accounting software, you can see where you're at financially, whenever you want to, wherever you are.

Get professional help

Accounts and tax returns can be complex to understand, especially for the first-time entrepreneur, and they're liable to change from year to year. Your time is better spent running the business rather than keeping up-to-date with the latest tax rates, laws and policies. Getting it wrong can mean hefty fines levied by the tax authorities. They don't accept ignorance or lack of knowledge as any excuse, so it's in your interest to hire a professional bookkeeper or accountant to make sure you meet your tax obligations.

A bookkeeper will provide continuing support with ongoing activities like following up on payments. They'll also provide sound advice on improving your accounting processes and systems to automate debtor management and financial reports, so you can keep a closer eye on your cash.

An accountant will prepare your end-of-financial year accounts and make sure you comply with tax requirements. A forward-looking accountant with access to your online accounts will also provide reports and advice on managing your finances and growing your business.

Plan and forecast

Try some simple forecasting – looking ahead for at least the next six months.

Be realistic and estimate how much you'll sell and how much you'll spend.

Your spending plan might look something like this:
- 50% of revenue on expenses such as payroll or supplies
- 30% of revenue on building the business – things like expansion of equipment or recruiting costs
- 20% of revenue on future development of new products and services

Plug the numbers into your financial plan and see if the results work for your business. If not, you may need to change your plan. And when circumstances change, your financial plan needs to change too.

If you're thinking of bidding for a big contract, stop and think about whether your cashflow will cover the costs of extra staff and equipment – and whether the time involved means you're likely to neglect existing clients. Also consider the effect on your cashflow if the new client is slow to pay, and when the contract ends.

Chart your cashflow

An easy way to chart your cashflow is to use accounting software. You can create charts of the money coming into your business from sales of goods or services and the money going out to pay the bills and other costs. It lets you change the time period and other variables so you can really understand what's happening. If you keep an eye on these charts over a period of weeks and months, you'll get an idea of how money flows in and out of your business.

Obviously, you need the inflows to be greater than the outflows to make a profit. But it's the size of the difference that matters. It will vary over time – some months or weeks will be good, some not so good. But looking at the charts will help you see patterns.

Is the difference between income and expenditure often small? Does it sometimes dip into negative territory? Those are periods when your business is at risk of cashflow problems. Try to see what causes this to happen and when. You can then attempt to re-organise some aspects of your business to avoid the dips.

Build a cash reserve
Aim to have enough cash on hand to last you around three to six months. That way, if you have a rough month or two, it shouldn't have a major effect on your business. A cash reserve provides a cushion to cope with unexpected events, economic ups and downs and changes in loan interest rates. It also gives you the confidence and finances to take advantage of growth opportunities for your business.

Building a cash reserve puts you in a position of strength. It might mean paying yourself a little less in the short term, but in the long term it will put your business on the path to success. That ultimately means more money in your pocket.

Make adjustments to regulate cashflow

If your cashflow is causing problems at specific times of the month or year, don't panic. You may be able to improve the situation without dramatic changes. You could:
● negotiate different payment dates with your suppliers to better align inflows with outflows
● shorten your invoicing payment terms to encourage your customers to

pay faster
- reduce the quantity of stock you hold – it costs you space and revenue
- establish a line of business credit so you can access extra money
- chase the money you're owed
- adjust your prices and margins
- review your expenses, loans and borrowing costs and see if they can be reduced – use your accounting software to generate reports related to your business expenditure, and in particular take a look at your profit and loss report, balance sheet, statement of cash flows, accounts payable and accounts receivable reports

Best practice invoicing for quicker payment

A product or service that's been delivered is the closest thing your business has to cold, hard cash. The sooner you invoice your client, the sooner you'll receive payment and the better it is for your cashflow.

If you've worked as an employee up to now, you'll be used to your pay arriving regularly in your account without having to think about it. Now, to get paid, you need to create and send invoices and follow up on unpaid ones. It's vital to get your invoicing process right from the start so it's efficient and pain-free, and your cashflow stays healthy.

Establish a relationship

It might seem like a small thing, but often introducing yourself to the people in the accounts departments of the companies you're invoicing can make a difference. All it takes is a polite phone call to let them know you're the primary contact for payment matters. At the same time, ask them to include your invoice number as a reference with every payment they make, to help you determine which invoice is being paid.

A small investment of your time talking to the person who makes the payments can prove invaluable. They're more likely to pay on time and it's easier to sort out any payment problems that arise.

Send invoices straight away

Once you've delivered a product or service, don't wait to invoice – get into the habit of sending invoices as soon as the job is done. Choose accounting software that has a mobile app so you can create and send your invoice while you're still on site or with your client.

If you're providing a service, think about asking for an initial payment upfront, a payment part-way through, or both. You could invoice for one-third upfront, one-third halfway through the job and one-third on completion. Or if the job is likely to be spread over months, it's reasonable to request payments at regular intervals (such as monthly) or at specified milestones.

These are things you'd agree with your customer before the job begins – and confirm in writing.   This way, if your customer runs into financial problems part-way through the project, you won't lose everything they owe you, or all the time and money you've spent doing the work. Be wary if a client insists on an invoicing interval that's longer than a month. Unless the circumstances clearly justify it, it could mean they have cashflow issues. You may want to do a credit check on them or talk to other suppliers before proceeding.

Surprisingly, some companies forget to invoice for smaller jobs due to pressure of work and being short on time. They may also leave it for weeks or months and then start going through their records to check what they're owed. This hurts cashflow – and it's avoidable. It can also make it awkward for your clients, especially if the invoice date is in a different tax year to when the work was done. Or your client might have assumed they're up-to-date with payments and may not have the funds available to pay you immediately.

Set up your invoices properly

Getting paid on time is harder if you don't set up your invoices properly. A professional invoice will include:
- full name and address of your business and your client
- invoice date and reference numbers
- name of the person responsible for processing the invoice
- sales taxes
- any legal requirements that apply, such as your company registration number, sales tax number, the registered company address, or all of these
- any discounts
- cost details including the number of items or hours/days chargeable, the cost per item or hour/day, the total amount for each entry, and the overall total
- invoice total – the amount payable including sales taxes and discounts (and specify the currency if there could be any doubt)
- invoice due date and any other payment terms such as a late fee
- payment methods you accept including your bank account details
- links to allow your customers to 'pay now' by PayPal or credit card if your
accounting software offers that option

Most accounting software will have templates to help you to set up invoices with all the necessary information in a professional-looking layout and your logo.

Keep accurate records

You can't invoice if you don't have accurate records of the work you've done for your customers. Keep track of the time and materials expended on a client's project and make sure you invoice for everything. Use time-tracking software and timesheets if you need to. Be sure to on-charge for materials and supplies you've purchased – some software will handle this for you. If you record the work done as you go, it saves you trying to remember the details at a later date and makes it less likely you'll forget something.

Define your payment terms

Very often, invoices are paid after the due date – especially in tough economic times. That's obviously not good for cashflow. Consider shortening your invoice payment period to encourage your customers to pay sooner. It's common for businesses to delay invoicing until the 20th of the month and expect payment 30 days later. But that's a corporate hangover and there's no need to wait this long to get paid.

You can set your payment period to one or two weeks. If you're serious about the work you do, and if you make your best efforts to supply your products and services to your clients' deadlines, there's no reason why they shouldn't try their best to pay you just as quickly.

Make sure you define your invoice payment terms clearly on all invoices – for example, 14 days from date of invoice. And include the actual due date for payment on the invoice – don't leave your clients to calculate when 14 days from the invoice date happens to be. You may like to offer a small discount for early payment. It sounds positive and is likely to be effective.

If you've set your payment terms out clearly on your invoice and the client has ignored them, in most countries you are entitled to charge interest in the form of a late payment fee. Be prepared for robust feedback from your clients if you go down this route, and consider reversing the charge once the lesson has been learned.

Offer easy payment methods

As a general rule, when you make it easier for your customers to pay, they'll pay sooner – and that's always a good outcome. Offer them choices of payment method if you can. While some payment methods mean extra fees for your business, you need to balance the costs against the ease of payment for your customers.

Some accounting software offers a 'pay now' button on online invoices. Your customers can pay there and then by credit card or PayPal. That means that you can send customers invoices online with the option of getting paid instantly.

Chase late payers

Once invoices have been issued, keep track of who's paid and who hasn't. Your accounting software will provide reports listing what you're owed from the oldest to the newest invoice, so you can see at a glance who owes you money and how much. Some accounting software also shows you if and when your customer opened the invoice online. Customers won't be able to pretend they haven't received your invoice when you can see they opened it weeks ago.

Some online accounting software allows you to set up automated invoice reminders. Gentle reminders can be emailed at intervals after the due date – or even before payment is due so you're more likely to get paid on time.

Using invoice reminders means you can set and forget about chasing payment until a point at which you've determined you need to contact the customer in person.

If you haven't got automated invoice reminders set up to do the work for you, then let the client know their account is overdue. Send a statement, a text message or an email.

Often that's all that's needed. But if the payment is a few weeks overdue, pick up the phone – reminders from a real person are much harder to ignore. Don't let it drift. Otherwise you may not get paid for ages, if at all.

Always be courteous when you chase the late payers as you want to maintain a working relationship. Keep in mind that you don't know their circumstances. A bereavement or other personal crisis may be the reason behind a normally reliable payer being late.

It can be difficult to proactively chase payment. You know you're owed the money, but actually asking for it can be stressful. However, your customer has taken your time and your product.

They have a legal and moral duty to pay you according to the agreed terms. So be resolute – courteous but firm.

Your clients aren't doing you a favour by paying – they must pay you, no matter how big or small they are.

And finally, don't be afraid to take more formal action through a debt collection agency or the courts if the situation comes to that.

Gary Turner

About the author

Gary is Xero's UK managing director. A 20-year veteran of the UK accounting software industry, he joined Xero from Microsoft where he was Product Group Director for Microsoft Dynamics. Gary has served on the IT Faculty Technical Committee of the Institute of Chartered Accountants of England and Wales since 2005.

25549170R00134

Printed in Poland
by Amazon Fulfillment
Poland Sp. z o.o., Wrocław